A SERIES OF

Lessons in Gnani Yoga

(The Yoga of Wisdom.)

A SERIES OF

Lessons in Gnani Yoga

(The Yoga of Wisdom.)

BY YOGI RAMACHARAKA

GYAN

Published by

Gyan Publishing House
5, Ansari Road
Daryaganj, New Delhi-110002
Phone: 011-47034999, 9811692060
E-mail: books@gyanbooks.com

Distribution Network
gyanbooks.com
India, USA, Canada, UK, Australia

ISBN: 978-93-6208-119-3 (PB)
First Published, 1906

2nd Impression 2024

Printed at: Gyan Press, Delhi.

A SERIES OF LESSONS IN GNANI YOGA (THE YOGA OF WISDOM)
Author: YOGI RAMACHARAKA

A SERIES OF

Lessons in Gnani Yoga

(The Yoga of Wisdom.)

By YOGI RAMACHARAKA.

THIS BOOK GIVES THE HIGHEST YOGI TEACHINGS REGARDING THE ABSOLUTE AND ITS MANIFESTATIONS.

THE YOGI PUBLICATION SOCIETY,
Chicago, Ill.

LONDON AGENTS:
L. N. FOWLER & Co., 7 Imperial Arcade, Ludgate Circus.

PUBLISHERS' NOTICE.

The lessons which compose this volume, originally appeared in the shape of monthly lessons, the first of which was issued in October, 1906, and the twelfth in September, 1907. These lessons met with a hearty and generous response from the public, and the present volume is issued in response to the demand for the lessons in a permanent and durable form. There have been no changes made in the text.

The publishers take the liberty to call the attention of the reader to the great amount of information condensed within the space given to each lesson. Students have told us that they have found it necessary to read and study each lesson carefully, in order to absorb the varied information contained within its pages. They have also stated that they have found it advisable to re-read the lessons several times, allowing an interval between each reading, and that at each re-reading they would discover information that had escaped them during the course of the previous study. This has been repeated to us so often that we feel justified in mentioning it, that other readers might avail themselves of the same course and plan of study.

Following his usual custom, the writer of the lessons has declined to write a preface for this book, claiming that the lessons speak for themselves, and that those for whom they are intended will receive the message contained within them, without any prefatory talk.

THE YOGI PUBLICATION SOCIETY.

September 1, 1907.

INDEX.

THE FIRST LESSON

The One.

The Yogi Philosophy may be divided into several great branches, or fields. What is known as "Hatha Yoga" deals with the physical body and its control; its welfare; its health; its preservation; its laws, etc. What is known as "Raja Yoga" deals with the Mind; its control; its development; its unfoldment, etc. What is known as "Bhakti Yoga" deals with the Love of the Absolute—God. What is known as "Gnani Yoga" deals with the scientific and intellectual knowing of the great questions regarding Life and what lies back of Life—the Riddle of the Universe.

Each branch of Yoga is but a path leading toward the one end—unfoldment, development, and growth. He who wishes first to develop, control and strengthen his physical body so as to render it a fit instrument of the Higher Self, follows the path of "Hatha Yoga." He who would develop his will-power and mental faculties, unfolding the inner senses, and latent powers, follows the path of "Raja Yoga." He who wishes to develop by "knowing"—by studying the fundamental principles, and the wonderful truths underlying Life, follows the path of "Gnani Yoga." And he who wishes to grow into a union with the One Life by the influence of Love, he follows the path of "Bhakti Yoga."

But it must not be supposed that the student must ally himself to only a single one of these paths to power. In fact, very few do. The majority prefer to gain a rounded knowledge, and acquaint themselves with the principles of the several branches, learning something of each, giving preference of course to those branches that appeal to them more strongly, this attraction being the indication of *need,* or requirement, and, therefore, being the hand pointing out the path.

It is well for every one to know something of "Hatha Yoga," in order that the body may be purified, strengthened, and kept in health in order to become a more fitting instrument of the Higher Self. It is well that each one should know something of "Raja Yoga," that he may understand the training and control of the mind, and the use of the Will. It is well that every one should learn the wisdom of "Gnani Yoga," that he may realize the wonderful truths underlying life—the science of Being. And, most assuredly every one should know something of Bhakti Yogi, that he may understand the great teachings regarding the Love underlying all life.

We have written a work on "Hatha Yoga," and a course on "Raja Yoga" which is now in book form. We have told you something regarding "Gnani Yoga" in our Fourteen Lessons, and also in our Advanced Course. We have written something regarding "Bhakti Yoga" in our Advanced Course, and, we hope, have taught it also all through our other lessons, for we fail to see how one can teach or study any of the branches of Yoga without being filled with a sense of Love and Union with the Source of all Life. To know the Giver of Life, is to love him, and the more we know of him, the more love will we manifest.

In this course of lessons, of which this is the first, we shall take up the subject of "Gnani Yoga"—the Yoga of Wisdom, and will endeavor to make plain some of its most important and highest teachings. And, we trust that in so doing, we shall be able to awaken in you a still higher realization of your relationship with the One, and a corresponding Love for that in which you live, and move and have your being. We ask for your loving sympathy and cooperation in our task.

Let us begin by a consideration of what has been called the "Questions of Questions"—the question: "What is Reality?" To understand the question we have but to take a look around us and view the visible world. We see great masses of something that science has called "matter." We see in operation a wonderful something called "force" or "energy" in its countless forms of manifestations. We see things that we call "forms of life," varying in manifestation from the tiny speck of slime that we call the Moneron, up to that form that we call Man.

But study this world of manifestations by means of science and research—and such study is of greatest value—still we must find ourselves brought to a point where we cannot progress further. Matter melts into mystery—Force resolves itself into something else—the secret of living-forms subtly elude us—and mind is seen as but the manifestation of something even finer. But in losing these things of appearance and manifestation, we find ourselves brought up face to face with a Something Else that we see must underlie all these varying forms, shapes and manifestations. And that Something Else, we call Reality, because it is Real, Permanent, Enduring. And although men may differ, dispute, wrangle, and quarrel about this Reality, still there is one point upon which they must agree, and that is that *Reality is One*—that underlying all forms and manifestations there must be a *One* Reality from which all things flow. And this inquiry into this One Reality is indeed the Question of Questions of the Universe.

The highest reason of Man—as well as his deepest intuition —has always recognized that this Reality or Underlying Being must be but ONE, of which all Nature is but varying degrees of manifestation, emanation, or expression. All have recognized that Life is a stream flowing from One great fount, the nature and name of which is unknown—some have said unknowable. Differ as men do about theories regarding the nature of this one, they all agree that it can be but One. It is only when men begin to name and analyze this One, that confusion results.

Let us see what men have thought and said about this One—it may help us to understand the nature of the problem.

The materialist claims that this one is a something called Matter—self-existent—eternal—infinite—containing within itself the potentiality of Matter, Energy and Mind. Another school, closely allied to the materialists, claim that this One is a something called Energy, of which Matter and Mind are but modes of motion. The Idealists claim that the One is a something called Mind, and that Matter and Force are but ideas in that One Mind. Theologians claim that this One is a something called a personal God, to whom they attribute certain qualities, characteristics, etc., the same varying with their creeds and dogmas. The Naturistic school claims that this One is a something called Nature, which is constantly manifesting itself in countless forms. The occultists, in their varying schools, Oriental and Occidental, have taught that the One was a Being whose Life constituted the life of all living forms.

All philosophies, all science, all religions, inform us that this world of shapes, forms and names is but a phenomenal or shadow world—a show-world—back of which rests Reality, called by some name of the teacher. But remember this, *all philosophy that counts* is based upon some form of monism—Oneness—whether the concept be a known or unknown god; an unknown or unknowable principle; a substance; an Energy, or Spirit. There is but One—there can be but One—such is the inevitable conclusion of the highest human reason, intuition or faith.

And, likewise, the same reason informs us that this One Life must permeate all apparent forms of life, and that all apparent material forms, forces, energies, and principles must be emanations from that One, and, consequently "of" it. It may be objected to, that the creeds teaching a personal god do not so hold, for they teach that their God is the creator of the Universe, which he has set aside from himself as a workman sets aside his workmanship. But this objection avails naught, for where could such a creator obtain the material for his universe, except from himself; and where the energy, except from the same source; and where the Life, unless from his One Life. So in the end, it is seen that there must be but One—not two, even if we prefer the terms God *and* his Universe, for even in this case the Universe must have proceeded from God, and can only live, and move and act, and think, by virtue of his Essence permeating it.

In passing by the conceptions of the various thinkers, we are struck by the fact that the various schools seem to manifest a one-sidedness in their theories, seeing only that which fits in with their theories, and ignoring the rest. The Materialist talks about Infinite and Eternal Matter, although the latest scientific investigations have shown us Matter fading into Nothingness—the Eternal Atom being split into countless particles called Corpuscles or Electrons, which at the last seem to be nothing but a unit of Electricity, tied up in a "knot in the Ether"—although just what the Ether is, Science does not dare to guess. And Energy, also seems to be unthinkable except as operating through matter, and always seems to be acting under the operation of Laws—and Laws without a

Law giver, and a Law giver without mind or something higher than Mind, is unthinkable. And Mind, as we know it, seems to be bound up with matter and energy in a wonderful combination, and is seen to be subject to laws outside of itself, and to be varying, inconstant, and changeable, which attributes cannot be conceived of as belonging to the Absolute. Mind as we know it, as well as Matter and Energy, is held by the highest occult teachers to be but an appearance and a relativity of something far more fundamental and enduring, and we are compelled to fall back upon that old term which wise men have used in order to describe that Something Else that lies back of, and under, Matter, Energy and Mind—and that word is "Spirit."

We cannot tell just what is meant by the word "Spirit," for we have nothing with which to describe it. But we can think of it as meaning the "essence" of Life and Being—the Reality underlying Universal Life.

Of course no name can be given to this One, that will fitly describe it. But we have used the term "The Absolute" in our previous lessons, and consider it advisable to continue its use, although the student may substitute any other name that appeals to him more strongly. We do not use the word God (except occasionally in order to bring out a shade of meaning) not because we object to it, but because by doing so we would run the risk of identifying The Absolute with some idea of a personal god with certain theological attributes. Nor does the word "Principle" appeal to us, for it seems to imply a cold, unfeeling, abstract thing, while we conceive the Absolute Spirit or Being to be a warm, vital, living, acting, feeling Reality. We do not use the word Nature, which many prefer, because of its materialistic meaning to the minds of many, although the word is very dear to us when referring to the outward manifestation of the Absolute Life.

Of the real nature of The Absolute, of course, we can know practically nothing, because it transcends all human experience and Man has nothing with which he can measure the Infinite. Spinoza was right when he said that "to define God is to deny him," for any attempt to define, is, of course an attempt to limit or make finite the Infinite. To define a thing is to identify it with something else—and where is the something else with which to identify the Infinite? The Absolute cannot be described in terms of the Relative. It is not Something, although it contains within itself the reality underlying Everything. It cannot be said to have the qualities of any of its apparently separated parts, for it is the ALL. It is all that really IS.

It is beyond Matter, Force, or Mind as we know it, and yet these things emanate from it, and must be within its nature. For what is in the manifested must be in the manifestor—no stream can rise higher than its source—the effect cannot be greater than the cause —you cannot get something out of nothing.

But it is hard for the human mind to take hold of

That which is beyond its experience—many philosophers consider it impossible—and so we must think of the Absolute in the concepts and terms of its highest manifestation. We find Mind higher in the scale than Matter or Energy, and so we are justified in using the terms of Mind in speaking of the Absolute, rather than the terms of Matter or Energy—so let us try to think of an Infinite Mind, whose powers and capacities are raised to an infinite degree—a Mind of which Herbert Spencer said that it was "a mode of being as much transcending intelligence and will, as these transcend mere mechanical motion."

While it is true (as all occultists know) that the best information regarding the Absolute come from regions of the Self higher than Intellect, yet we are in duty bound to examine the reports of the Intellect concerning its information regarding the One. The Intellect has been developed in us for use—for the purpose of examining, considering, thinking—and it behooves us to employ it. By turning it to this purpose, we not only strengthen and unfold it, but we also get certain information that can reach us by no other channel. And moreover, by such use of the Intellect we are able to discover many fallacies and errors that have crept into our minds from the opinions and dogmas of others—as Kant said: "The chief, and perhaps the only, use of a philosophy of pure reason is a negative one. It is not an organon for extending, but a discipline for limiting! Instead of discovering truth, its modest function is to guard against error." Let us then listen to the report of the Intellect, as well as of the higher fields of mentation.

One of the first reports of the Intellect, concerning the Absolute, is that it must have existed forever, and must continue to exist forever. There is no escape from this conclusion, whether one view the matter from the viewpoint of the materialist, philosopher, occultist, or theologian. The Absolute could not have sprung from Nothing, and there was no other cause outside of itself from which it could have emanated. And there can be no cause outside of itself which can terminate its being. And we cannot conceive of Infinite Life, or Absolute Life, dying. So the Absolute must be Eternal—such is the report of the Intellect.

This idea of the Eternal is practically unthinkable to the human mind, although it is forced to believe that it must be a quality of the Absolute. The trouble arises from the fact that the Intellect is compelled to see everything through the veil of Time, and Cause and Effect. Now, Cause and Effect, and Time, are merely phenomena or appearances of the relative world, and have no place in the Absolute and Real. Let us see if we can understand this.

Reflection will show you that the only reason that you are unable to think of or picture a Causeless Cause, is because everything that you have experienced in this relative world of the senses has had a cause—something from which it sprung. You have seen Cause and Effect in full operation all about you, and quite naturally your Intellect has taken it for granted that there can be nothing uncaused—nothing without a preceding cause. And the Intellect is perfectly right, so far as Things are concerned, for all Things are relative and are therefore caused. But back of the caused things must lie THAT which is the Great Causer of Things, and which, not being a Thing itself, cannot have been caused—cannot be the effect of a cause. Your minds reel when you try to form a mental image of That which has had no cause, because you have had no experience in the sense world of such a thing, and there fail to form the image. It is out of your experience, and you cannot form the mental picture. But yet your mind is compelled to believe that there must have been an Original One, that can have had no cause. This is a hard task for the Intellect, but in time it comes to see just where the trouble lies, and ceases to interpose objections to the voice of the higher regions of the self.

And, the Intellect experiences a similar difficulty when it tries to think of an Eternal—a That which is above and outside of Time. We see Time in operation everywhere, and take it for granted that Time is a reality—an actual thing. But this is a mistake of the senses. There is no such thing as Time, in reality. Time exists solely in our minds. It is merely a form of perception by which we express our consciousness of the Change in Things.

We cannot think of Time except in connection with a succession of changes of things in our consciousness

—either things of the outer world, or the passing of thought-things through our mind. A day is merely the consciousness of the passing of the sun—an hour or minute merely the subdivision of the day, or else the consciousness of the movement of the hands of the clock—merely the consciousness of the movement of Things—the symbols of changes in Things. In a world without changes in Things, there would be no such thing as Time. Time is but a mental invention. Such is the report of the Intellect.

And, besides the conclusions of pure abstract reasoning about Time, we may see many instances of the relativity of Time in our everyday experiences. We all know that when we are interested Time seems to pass rapidly, and when we are bored it drags along in a shameful manner. We know that when we are happy, Time develops the speed of a meteor, while when we are unhappy it crawls like a tortoise. When we are interested or happy our attention is largely diverted from the changes occurring in things—because we do not notice the Things so closely. And while we are miserable or bored, we notice the details in Things, and their changes, until the length of time seems interminable. A tiny insect mite may, and does, live a lifetime of birth, growth, marriage, reproduction, old age, and death, in a few minutes, and no doubt its life seems as full as does that of the elephant with his hundred years. Why? *Because so many things have happened!* When we are conscious of many things happening, we get the impression and sensation of the length of time. The greater the consciousness of things, the greater the sensation of Time. When we are so interested in talking to a loved one that we forget all that is occurring about us, then the hours fly by unheeded, while the same hours seem like days to one in the same place who is not interested or occupied with some task.

Men have nodded, and in the second before awakening they have dreamed of events that seemed to have required the passage of years. Many of you have had experiences of this kind, and many such cases have been recorded by science. On the other hand, one may fall asleep and remain unconscious, but without dreams, for hours, and upon awakening will insist that he has merely nodded. Time belongs to the relative mind, and has no place in the Eternal or Absolute.

Next, the Intellect informs us that it must think of the Absolute as Infinite in Space—present everywhere—Omnipresent. It cannot be limited, for there is nothing outside of itself to limit it. There is no such place as Nowhere. Every place is in the Everywhere. And Everywhere is filled with the All—the Infinite Reality—the Absolute.

And, just as was the case with the idea of Time, we find it most difficult—if not indeed impossible—to form an idea of an Omnipresent—of That which occupies Infinite Space. This because everything that our minds have experienced has had dimensions and limits. The secret lies in the fact that Space, like

Time, has no real existence outside of our perception of consciousness of the relative position of Things—material objects. We see this thing here, and that thing there. Between them is Nothingness. We take another object, say a yard-stick, and measure off this Nothingness between the two objects, and we call this measure of Nothingness by the term Distance. And yet we cannot have measured Nothingness—that is impossible. What have we really done? Simply this, determined how many lengths of yard-stick could be laid between the other two objects.

We call this process measuring Space, but Space is Nothing, and we have merely determined the relative position of objects. To "measure Space" we must have three Things or objects, *i. e.*, (1) The object from which we start the measure; (2) The object with which we measure; and (3) The object with which we end our measurement. We are unable to conceive of Infinite Space, because we lack the third object in the measuring process—the ending object. We may use ourselves as a starting point, and the mental yard-stick is always at hand, but where is the object at the other side of Infinity of Space by which the measurement may be ended? It is not there, and we cannot think of the end without it.

Let us start with ourselves, and try to imagine a million million miles, and then multiply them by another million million miles, a million million times. What have we done? Simply extended our mental yard-stick a certain number of times to an imaginary point in the Nothingness that we call Space. So far so good, but the mind intuitively recognizes that beyond that imaginary point at the end of the last yard-stick, there is a capacity for an infinite extension of yard-sticks—an infinite capacity for such extension. Extension of what? Space? No! Yard-sticks! Objects! Things! Without material objects Space is unthinkable. It has no existence outside of our consciousness of Things. There is no such thing as Real Space. Space is merely an infinite capacity for extending objects. Space itself is merely a name for Nothingness. If you can form an idea of an object swept out of existence, and nothing to take its place, that Nothing would be called Space, the term implying the possibility of placing something there without displacing anything else.

Size, of course, is but another form of speaking of Distance. And in this connection let us not forget that just as one may think of Space being infinite in the direction of largeness, so may we think of it as being infinite in the sense of smallness. No matter how small may be an object thought of, we are still able to think of it as being capable of subdivision, and so on infinitely. There is no limit in this direction either. As Jakob has said: "The conception of the infinitely minute is as little capable of being grasped by us, as is that of the infinitely great. Despite this, the admission of the reality of the infinitude, both in the direction of greatness and of minuteness, is inevitable."

And, as Radenhausen has said: "The idea of Space is only an unavoidable illusion of our Consciousness, or of our finite nature, and does not exist outside of ourselves; the universe is infinitely small and infinitely great."

The telescope has opened to us ideas of magnificent vastness and greatness, and the perfected microscope has opened to us a world of magnificent smallness and minuteness. The latter has shown us that a drop of water is a world of minute living forms who live, eat, fight, reproduce, and die. The mind is capable of imagining a universe occupying no more space than one million-millionth of the tiniest speck visible under the strongest microscope—and then imagining such a universe containing millions of suns and worlds similar to our own, and inhabited by living forms akin to ours—living, thinking men and women, identical in every respect to ourselves. Indeed, as some philosophers have said, if our Universe were suddenly reduced to such a size—the relative proportions of everything being preserved, of course—then we would not be conscious of any change, and life would go on the same, and we would be of the same importance to ourselves and to the Absolute as we are this moment. And the same would be true were the Universe suddenly enlarged a million-million times. These changes would make no difference in reality. Compared with each other, the tiniest speck and the largest sun are practically the same size when viewed from the Absolute.

We have dwelt upon these things so that you would be able to better realize the relativity of Space and Time, and perceive that they are merely symbols of Things used by the mind in dealing with finite objects, and have no place in reality. When this is realized, then the idea of Infinity in Time and Space is more readily grasped.

As Radenhausen says: "Beyond the range of human reason there is neither Space nor Time; they are arbitrary conceptions of man, at which he has arrived by the comparison and arrangement of different impressions which he has received from the outside world. The conception of Space arises from the sequence of the various forms which fill Space, by which the external world appears to the individual man. The conception of Time arises from the sequence of the various forms which change in space (motion), by which the external world acts on the individual man, and so on. But externally to ourselves, the distinction between repletion of Space and mutation of Space does not exist, for each is in constant transmutation, whatever is is filling and changing at the same time—nothing is at a standstill," and to quote Ruckert: "The world has neither beginning nor end, in space nor in time. Everywhere is center and turning-point, and in a moment is eternity."

Next, the Intellect informs us that we must think of the Absolute as containing within Itself all the Power there is, because there can be no other source or reservoir of Power, and there can be no Power outside of the All-Power. There can be no Power outside of the Absolute to limit, confine, or conflict with It. Any laws of the Universe must have been imposed by It, for there is no other law-giver, and every manifestation of Energy, Force, or Power, perceived or evident in Nature must be a part of the Power of the Absolute working along lines laid down by it. In the Third Lesson, which will be entitled The Will-to-Live, we shall see this Power manifesting along the lines of Life as we know it.

Next, the Intellect informs us that it is compelled to think of the Absolute as containing within Itself all possible Knowledge or Wisdom, because there can be no Knowledge or Wisdom outside of It, and therefore all the Wisdom and Knowledge possible must be within It. We see Mind, Wisdom, and Knowledge manifested by relative forms of Life, and such must emanate from the Absolute in accordance with certain laws laid down by It, for otherwise there would be no such wisdom, etc., for there is nowhere outside of the All from whence it could come. The effect cannot be greater than the cause. If there is anything unknown to the Absolute, then it will never be known to finite minds. So, therefore, ALL KNOWLEDGE that Is, Has Been, or Can Be, must be NOW vested in the One—the Absolute.

This does not mean that the Absolute *thinks,* in any such sense as does Man. The Absolute must Know, without Thinking. It does not have to gather Knowledge by the process of Thinking, as does Man—such an idea would be ridiculous, for from whence could the Knowledge come outside of itself. When man thinks he draws to himself Knowledge from the Universal source by the action of the Mind, but the Absolute has only itself to draw on. So we cannot imagine the Absolute compelled to Think as we do.

But, lest we be misunderstood regarding this phase of the subject, we may say here that the highest occult teachings inform us that the Absolute *does* manifest a quality somewhat akin to what we would call constructive thought, and that such "thoughts" manifest into objectivity and manifestation, and become Creation. Created Things, according to the Occult teachings are "Thoughts of God." Do not let this idea disturb you, and cause you to feel that you are nothing, because you have been called into being by a Thought of the Infinite One. Even a Thought of that One would be intensely real in the relative world—actually Real to all except the Absolute itself—and even the Absolute knows that the *Real* part of its Creations must be a part of itself manifested through its thought, for the Thought of the Infinite must be Real, and a part of Itself, for it cannot be anything else, and to call it Nothing is merely to juggle with words. The faintest Thought of the Infinite One would be far more real than anything man could create—as solid as the mountain—as hard as steel—as durable as the diamond—for, verily, even these are emanations of the Mind of the Infinite, and are things of but a day, while the higher Thoughts—

the soul of Man—contains within itself a spark from the Divine Flame itself—the Spirit of the Infinite. But these things will appear in their own place, as we proceed with this series. We have merely given you a little food for thought at this point, in connection with the Mind of the Absolute.

So you see, good friends and students, that the Intellect in its highest efforts, informs us that it finds itself compelled to report that the One—the Absolute—That which it is compelled to admit really exists—must be a One possessed of a nature so far transcending human experience that the human mind finds itself without the proper concepts, symbols, and words with which to think of It. But none the less, the Intellect finds itself bound by its own laws to postulate the existence of such an One.

It is the veriest folly to try to think of the One as It is "in Itself"—for we have nothing but human attributes with which to measure it, and It so far transcends such measurements that the mental yardsticks run out into infinity and are lost sight of. The highest minds of the race inform us that the most exalted efforts of their reason compels them to report that the One—in Itself—cannot be spoken of as possessing attributes or qualities capable of being expressed in human words employed to describe the Things of the relative world—and all of our words are such. All of our words originate from such ideas, and all of our ideas arise from our experience, directly or indirectly. So we are not equipped with words with which to think of or speak of that which transcends experience, although our Intellect informs us that Reality lies back of our experience.

Philosophy finds itself unable to do anything better than to bring us face to face with high paradoxes. Science in its pursuit of Truth finds it cunningly avoiding it, and ever escaping its net. And we believe that the Absolute purposely causes this to be, that in the end Man may be compelled to look for the Spirit within himself—the only place where he can come in touch with it. This, we think, is the answer to the Riddle of the Sphinx—"Look Within for that which Thou needest."

But while the Spirit may be discerned only by looking within ourselves, we find that once the mind realizes that the Absolute Is, it will be able to see countless evidences of its action and presence by observing manifested Life without. All Life is filled with the Life Power and Will of the Absolute.

To us Life is but One—the Universe is a living Unity, throbbing, thrilling and pulsating with the Will-to-Live of the Absolute. Back of all apparent shapes, forms, names, forces, elements, principles and substances, there is but One—One Life, present everywhere, and manifesting in an infinitude of shapes, forms, and forces. All individual lives are but centers of consciousness in the One Life underlying, depending upon it for degree of unfoldment, expression and manifestation.

This may sound like Pantheism to some, but it is

very different from the Pantheism of the schools and cults. Pantheism is defined as "the doctrine that God consists in the combined forces and laws manifested in the existing Universe," or that "the Universe taken or conceived as a whole is God." These definitions do not fit the conception of the Absolute, of the Yogi Philosophy—they seem to breathe but a refined materialism. The Absolute is not "the combined forces and laws manifested in the universe," nor "the universe conceived as a whole." Instead, the Universe, its forces and laws, even conceived as a whole, have no existence in themselves, but are mere manifestations of the Absolute. Surely this is different from Pantheism.

We teach that the Absolute is immanent in, and abiding in all forms of Life in the Universe, as well as in its forces and laws—all being but manifestations of the Will of the One. And we teach that this One is superior to all forms of manifestations, and that Its existence and being does not depend upon the manifestations, which are but effects of the Cause.

The Pantheistic Universe—God is but a thing of phenomenal appearance, but the Absolute is the very Spirit of Life—a Living, Existing Reality, and would be so even if every manifestation were withdrawn from appearance and expression—drawn back into the source from which it emanated. The Absolute is more than Mountain or Ocean—Electricity or Gravitation—Monad or Man—It is SPIRIT—LIFE—BE-

ING—REALITY—the ONE THAT IS. Omnipotent, Omnipresent; Omniscient; Eternal; Infinite; Absolute; these are Man's greatest words, and yet they but feebly portray a shadow thrown by the One Itself.

The Absolute is not a far-away Being directing our affairs at long range—not an absentee Deity—but an Immanent Life in and about us all—manifesting in us and creating us into individual centers of consciousness, in pursuance with some great law of being.

And, more than this, the Absolute instead of being an indiffrent and unmoved spectator to its own creation, is a thriving, longing, active, suffering, rejoicing, feeling Spirit, partaking of the feelings of its manifestations, rather than callously witnessing them. It lives in us—with us—through us. Back of all the pain in the world may be found a great feeling and suffering love. The pain of the world is not punishment or evidence of divine wrath, but the incidents of the working out of some cosmic plan, in which the Absolute is the Actor, through the forms of Its manifestations.

The message of the Absolute to some of the Illumined has been, "All is being done in the best and only possible way—I am doing the best I can—all is well—and in the end will so appear."

The Absolute is no personal Deity—yet in itself it contains all that goes to make up all personality and all human relations. Father, Mother, Child, Friend, Lover—all is in It. All forms of human love and craving for sympathy, understanding and companionship may find refuge in loving the Absolute.

The Absolute is constantly in evidence in our lives, and yet we have been seeking it here and there in the outer world, asking it to show itself and prove Its existence. Well may it say to us: "Hast thou been so long time with me, and hast thou not known me?" This is the great tragedy of Life, that the Spirit comes to us—Its own—and we know It not. We fail to hear Its words: "Oh, ye who mourn, I suffer with you and through you. Yea, it is I who grieve in you. Your pain is mine—to the last pang. I suffer all pain through you—and yet I rejoice beyond you, for I know that through you, and with you, I shall conquer."

And this is a faint idea of what we believe the Absolute to be. In the following lessons we shall see it in operation in all forms of life, and in ourselves. We shall get close to the workings of Its mighty Will—close to Its Heart of Love.

Carry with you the Central Thought of the Lesson:

CENTRAL THOUGHT. There is but One Life in the Universe. And underlying that One Life—Its Real Self—Its Essence—Its Spirit—is The Absolute, living, feeling, suffering, rejoicing, longing, striving, in and through us. The Absolute is all that really Is, and all the visible Universe and forms of Life is Its expression, through Its Will. We lack words adequate to describe the nature of the Absolute, but we will use two words describing its inmost nature as best we see it. These two words are LIFE and LOVE, the one describing the outer, the other the inner nature. Let us manifest both Life and Love as a token of our origin and inner nature. Peace be with you.

THE SECOND LESSON

Omnipresent Life.

In our First Lesson of this series, we brought out the idea that the human mind was compelled to report the fact that it could not think of The Absolute except as possessing the quality of Omnipresence—Present-Everywhere. And, likewise, the human mind is compelled to think that all there IS must be The Absolute, or *of* the Absolute. And if a thing is *of* the Absolute, then the Absolute must be *in* it, in some way—must be the *essence* of it. Granting this, we must then think that everything must be filled with the essence of Life, for Life must be one of the qualities of the Absolute, or rather what we call Life must be the outward expression of the essential Being of the Absolute. And if this be so, then it would follow that *everything in the Universe must be Alive.* The mind cannot escape this conclusion. And if the facts do not bear out this conclusion then we must be forced to admit that the entire basic theory of the Absolute and its emanations must fall, and be considered as an error. No chain is stronger than its weakest link, and if this link be too weak to bear the weight of the facts of the universe, then must the chain be discarded as imperfect and useless, and another substituted. This fact is not generally mentioned by those speaking and writing of All being One, or an emanation of the One, but it must be considered and met. If there is a single thing in the Universe that is "dead"—non-living—lifeless—then the theory must fall. If a thing is non-living, then the essence of the Absolute cannot be in it—it must be alien and foreign to the Absolute, and in that case the Absolute cannot be Absolute for there is something outside of itself. And so it becomes of the greatest importance to examine into the evidences of the presence of Life in all things, organic or inorganic. The evidence is at hand—let us examine it.

The ancient occultists of all peoples always taught that the Universe was Alive—that there was Life in everything—that there was nothing dead in Nature—that Death meant simply a change in form in the material of the dead bodies. They taught that Life, in varying degrees of manifestation and expression, was present in everything and object, even down to the hardest mineral form, and the atoms composing that form.

Modern Science is now rapidly advancing to the same position, and each months investigations and discoveries serve only to emphasize the teachings.

Burbank, that wonderful moulder of plant life, has well expressed this thought, when he says: "All my investigations have led me away from the idea of a dead material universe tossed about by various forces, to that of a universe which is absolutely all force, life, soul, thought, or whatever name we may choose to call it. Every atom, molecule, plant, animal or planet, is only an aggregation of organized unit forces, held in place by stronger forces, thus holding them for a time latent, though teeming with inconceivable power. All life on our planet is, so to speak, just on the outer fringe of this infinite ocean of force. The universe is not half dead, but all alive."

Science today is gazing upon a living universe. She has not yet realized the full significance of what she has discovered, and her hands are raised as if to shade her eyes from the unaccustomed glare that is bursting upon her. From the dark cavern of universal dead matter, she has stepped out into the glare of the noonday sun of a Universe All-Alive even to its smallest and apparently most inert particle.

Beginning at Man, the highest form of Life known to us, we may pass rapidly down the scale of animal life, seeing life in full operation at each descending step. Passing from the animal to the vegetable kingdom, we still see Life in full operation, although in lessened degrees of expression. We shall not stop here to review the many manifestations of Life among the forms of plant-life, for we shall have occasion to mention them in our next lesson, but it must be apparent to all that Life is constantly manifesting in the sprouting of seeds; the putting forth of stalk, leaves, blossoms, fruit, etc., and in the enormous manifestation of force and energy in such growth and development. One may see the life force in the plant pressing forth for expression and manifestation, from the first sprouting of the seed, until the last vital action on the part of the mature plant or tree.

Besides the vital action observable in the growth and development of plants, we know, of course, that plants sicken and die, and manifest all other attributes of living forms. There is no room for argument about the presence of life in the plant kingdom.

But there are other forms of life far below the scale of the plants. There is the world of the bacteria, microbes, infusoria—the groups of cells with a common life—the single cell creatures, down to the Monera, the creatures lower than the single cells—the Things of the slime of the ocean bed.

These tiny Things—living Things—present to the sight merely a tiny speck of jelly, without organs of any kind. And yet they exercise all the functions of life—movement, nutrition, reproduction, sensation, and dissolution. Some of these elementary forms are all stomach, that is they are all one organ capable of performing all the functions necessary for the life of the animal. The creature has no mouth, but when it wishes to devour an object it simply envelopes it—wraps itself around it like a bit of glue around a gnat, and then absorbs the substance of its prey through its whole body.

Scientists have turned some of these tiny creatures inside out, and yet they have gone on with their life functions undisturbed and untroubled. They have cut them up into still tinier bits, and yet each bit lived on as a separate animal, performing all of its functions undisturbed. They are all the same all over, and all the way through. They reproduce themselves by growing to a certain size, and then separating into two, and so on. The rapidity of the increase is most remarkable.

Haekel says of the Monera: "The Monera are the simplest permanent cytods. Their entire body consists of merely soft, structureless plasm. However thoroughly we may examine them with the help of the most delicate reagents and the strongest optical instruments, we yet find that all the parts are completely homogeneous. These Monera are therefore, in the strictest sense of the word, 'organisms without organs,' or even in a strict philosophical sense they might not even be called organisms, since they possess no organs and since they are not composed of various particles. They can only be called organisms in so far as they are capable of exercising the organic phenomena of life, of nutrition, reproduction, sensation and movement."

Verworn records an interesting instance of life and mind among the *Rhizopods,* a very low form of living thing. He relates that the *Difflugia ampula,* a creature occupying a tiny shell formed of minute particles of sand, has a long projection of its substance, like a feeler or tendril, with which it searches on the bottom of the sea for sandy material with which to build the shell or outer covering for its offspring, which are born by division from the parent body. It grasps the particle of sand by the feeler, and passes it into its body by enclosing it. Verworn removed the sand from the bottom of the tank, replacing it by very minute particles of highly colored glass. Shortly afterward he noticed a collection of these particles of glass in the body of the creature, and a little later he saw a tiny speck of protoplasm emitted from the parent by separation. At the same time he noticed that the bits of glass collected by the mother creature were passed out and placed around the body of the new creature, and cemented together by a substance secreted by the body of the parent, thus forming a shell and covering for the offspring. This proceeding showed the presence of a mental something sufficient to cause the creature to prepare a shell for the offspring previous to its birth—or rather to gather the material for such shell, to be afterward used; to distinguish the proper material; to mould it into shape, and cement it. The scientist reported that a creature always gathered just exactly enough sand for its purpose—never too little, and never an excess. And this in a creature that is little more than a tiny drop of glue!

We may consider the life actions of the Moneron a little further, for it is the lowest form of so-called "living matter"—the point at which living forms pass off into non-living forms (so-called). This tiny speck of glue—an organism without organs—is endowed with the faculty called sensation. It draws away from that which is likely to injure it, and toward that which it desires—all in response to an elementary sensation. It has the instinct of self-preservation and self-protection. It seeks and finds its prey, and then eats, digests and assimilates it. It is able to move about by "false-feet," or bits of its body which it pushes forth at will from any part of its substance. It reproduces itself, as we have seen, by separation and self-division.

The life of the bacteria and germs—the yeasty forms of life—are familiar to many of us. And yet there are forms of life still below these. The line between living forms and non-living forms is being set back further and further by science. Living creatures are now known that resemble the non-living so closely that the line cannot be definitely drawn.

Living creatures are known that are capable of being dried and laid away for several years, and then may be revived by the application of moisture. They resemble dust, but are full of life and function. Certain forms of bacilli are known to Science that have been subjected to degrees of heat and cold that are but terms to any but the scientific mind.

Low forms of life called Diatoms or "living crystals" are known. They are tiny geometrical forms. They are composed of a tiny drop of plasm, resembling glue, covered by a thin shell of siliceous or sandy material. They are visible only through the microscope, and are so small that thousands of them might be gathered together on the head of a pin. They are so like chemical crystals that it requires a shrewd and careful observer to distinguish them. And yet they are alive, and perform all the functions of life.

Leaving these creatures, we enter the kingdom of the crystals, in our search for life. Yes, the crystals manifest life, as strange as this statement may appear to those who have not followed the march of Science. The crystals are born, grow, live, and may be killed by chemicals or electricity. Science has added a new department called "Plasmology," the purpose of which is the study of crystal life. Some investigators have progressed so far as to claim that they have discovered signs of rudimentary sex functioning among crystals. At any rate, crystals are born and grow like living things. As a recent scientific writer has said: "Crystallization, as we are to learn now, is not a mere mechanical grouping of dead atoms. It is a birth."

The crystal forms from the mother liquor, and its body is built up systematically, regularly, and according to a well defined plan or pattern, just as are the body and bones of the animal form, and the wood and bark of the tree. There is life at work in the growth of the crystal. And not only does the crystal grow, but it also reproduces itself by separation or splitting-off, just as is the case with the lower forms of life, just mentioned.

The principal point of difference between the growth and development of the crystals and that of the lower forms of life referred to is that the crystal takes its nourishment from the outside, and builds up from its outer surface, while the Monera absorbs its nourishment from within, and grows outwardly from within. If the crystal had a soft center, and took its nourishment in that way, it would be almost identical with the Diatom, or, if the Diatom grew from the outside, it would be but a crystal. A very fine dividing line.

Crystals, like living forms, may be sterilized and rendered incapable of reproduction by chemical process, or electrical discharges. They may also be "killed" and future growth prevented in this manner. Surely this looks like "Life," does it not?

To realize the importance of this idea of life among the crystals, we must remember that our hardest rocks and metals are composed of crystals, and that the dirt and earth upon which we grow and live are but crumbled rock and miniature crystals. Therefore the very dust under our feet is alive. *There is nothing dead.* There is no transformation of "dead matter" into live plant matter, and then into live animal matter. The chemicals are alive, and from chemical to man's body there is but a continuous change of shape and form of living matter. Any man's body, decomposing, is again resolved into chemicals, and the chain begins over again. Merely changes in living forms—that's all, so far as the bodies are concerned.

Nature furnishes us with many examples of this presence of life in the inorganic world. We have but to look around to see the truth of the statement that All is Alive. There is that which is known as the "fatigue of elasticity" in metals. Razors get tired, and require a rest. Tuning forks lose their powers of vibration, to a degree, and have to be given a vacation. Machinery in mills and manufactories needs an occasional day off. Metals are subject to disease and infection, and have been poisoned and restored by antidotes. Window glass, especially stained glass, is subject to a disease spreading from pane to pane.

Men accustomed to handling and using tools and machinery naturally drop into the habit of speaking of these things as if they were alive. They seem to recognize the presence of "feeling" in tools or machine, and to perceive in each a sort of "character" or personality, which must be respected, humored, or coaxed in order to get the best results.

Perhaps the most valuable testimony along these lines, and which goes very far toward proving the centuries-old theories of the Yogis regarding Omnipresent Life, comes from Prof. J. Chunder Bose, of the Calcutta University, a Hindu educated in the English Universities, under the best teachers, and who is now a leading scientific authority in the western world. He has given to the world some very valuable scientific information along these lines in his book entitled "*Response in the Living and Non-living,*" which has caused the widest comment and created the greatest interest among the highest scientific authorities. His experiments along the lines of the gathering of evidence of life in the inorganic forms have revolutionized the theories of modern science, and have done much to further the idea that life is present everywhere, and that there is no such thing as dead matter.

He bases his work upon the theory that the best and only true test for the presence of life in matter is the response of matter to external stimulus. Proceeding from this fundamental theory he has proven by innumerable experiments that so-called inorganic matter, minerals, metals, etc., give a response to such stimulus, which response is similar, if not identical, to the response of the matter composing the bodies of plants, animals, men.

He devised delicate apparatus for the measurement of the response to the outside stimulus, the degree, and other evidence being recorded in traces on a revolving cylinder. The tracings or curves obtained from tin and other metals, when compared with those obtained from living muscle, were found to be identical. He used a galvanometer, a very delicate and accurate scientific instrument, in his experiments. This instrument is so finely adjusted that the faintest current will cause a deflection of the registering needle, which is delicately swung on a tiny pivot. If the galvanometer be attached to a human nerve, and the end of the nerve be irritated, the needle will register.

Prof. Bose found that when he attached the galvanometer to bars of various metals they gave a similar response when struck or twisted. The greater the irritation applied to the metal, the greater the response registered by the instrument. The analogy between the response of the metal and that of the living muscle was startling. For instance, just as in the case of the living animal muscle or nerve matter, the response becomes fatigued, so in the case of the metal the curve registered by the needle became fainter and still fainter, as the bar became more and more fatigued by the continued irritation. And again, just after such fatigue the muscle would become rested, and would again respond actively, so would the metal when given a chance to recuperate.

Tetanus due to shocks constantly repeated, was caused and recovered. Metals recorded evidences of fatigue. Drugs caused identical effects on metals and animals—some exciting; some depressing; some killing. Some poisonous chemicals killed pieces of metal, rendering them immobile and therefore incapable of registering records on the apparatus. In some cases antidotes were promptly administered, and saved the life of the metal.

Prof. Bose also conducted experiments on plants in the same way. Pieces of vegetable matter were found to be capable of stimulation, fatigue, excitement, depression, poison. Mrs. Annie Besant, who witnessed some of these experiments in Calcutta, has written as follows regarding the experiments on plant life: "There is something rather pathetic in seeing the way in which the tiny spot of light which records the pulses in the plant, travels in ever weaker and weaker curves, when the plant is under the influence of poison, then falls into a final despairing straight line, and—stops. One feels as though a murder has been committed—as indeed it has."

In one of Prof. Bose's public experiments he clearly demonstrated that a bar of iron was fully as sensitive as the human body, and that it could be irritated and stimulated in the same way, and finally could be poisoned and killed. "Among such phenomena," he asks, "how can we draw the line of demarkation, and say, 'Here the physical ends, and there the physiological begins'? No such barrier exists." According to his theory, which agrees with the oldest occult theories, by the way, life is present in every object and form of Nature, and all forms respond to external stimulus, which response is a proof of the presence of life in the form.

Prof. Bose's great book is full of the most startling results of experiments. He proves that the metals manifest something like sleep; can be killed; exhibit torpor and sluggishness; get tired or lazy; wake up; can be roused into activity; may be stimulated, strengthened, weakened; suffer from extreme cold and heat; may be drugged or intoxicated, the different metals manifesting a different response to certain drugs, just as different men and animals manifest a varying degree of similar resistance. The response of a piece of steel subjected to the influence of a chemical poison shows a gradual fluttering and weakening until it finally dies away, just as animal matter does when similarly poisoned. When revived in time by an antidote, the recovery was similarly gradual in both metal and muscle. A remarkable fact is noted by the scientist when he tells us that the very poisons that kill the metals are themselves alive and may be killed, drugged, stimulated, etc., showing the same response as in the case of the metals, proving the existence in them of the same life that is in the metals and animal matter that they influence.

Of course when these metals are "killed" there is merely a killing of the metal as metal—the atoms and principles of which the metal is composed remaining fully alive and active, just as is the case with the atom of the human body after the soul passes out—

the body is as much alive after death as during the life of the person, the activity of the parts being along the lines of dissolution instead of construction in that case.

We hear much of the claims of scientists who announce that they are on the eve of "*creating* life" from non-living matter. This is all nonsense—life can come only from life. Life from non-life is an absurdity. And all Life comes from the One Life underlying All. But it is true that Science has done, is doing, and will do, something very much like "creating life," but of course this is merely changing the form of Life into other forms—the lesser form into the higher—just as one produces a plant from a seed, or a fruit from a plant. The Life is always there, and responds to the proper stimulus and conditions.

A number of scientists are working on the problem of generating living forms from inorganic matter. The old idea of "spontaneous generation," for many years relegated to the scrap-pile of Science, is again coming to the front. Although the theory of Evolution compels its adherents to accept the idea that at one time in the past living forms sprung from the non-living (so-called), yet it has been generally believed that the conditions which brought about this stage of evolution has forever passed. But the indications now all point to the other view that this stage of evolution is, and always has been, in operation, and that new forms of life are constantly evolving from the inorganic forms. "Creation," so-called (although the word is an absurdity from the Yogi point of view), is constantly being performed.

Dr. Charlton Bastian, of London, Eng., has long been a prominent advocate of this theory of continuous spontaneous generation. Laughed down and considered defeated by the leading scientific minds of a generation ago, he still pluckily kept at work, and his recent books were like bombshells in the orthodox scientific camp. He has taken more than five thousand photo-micrographs, all showing most startling facts in connection with the origin of living forms from the inorganic. He claims that the microscope reveals the development in a previously clear liquid of very minute black spots, which gradually enlarge and transform into bacteria—living forms of a very low order. Prof. Burke, of Cambridge, Eng., has demonstrated that he may produce in sterilized boullion, subjected to the action of sterilized radium chloride, minute living bodies which manifest growth and subdivision. Science is being gradually forced to the conclusion that living forms are still arising in the world by natural processes, which is not at all remarkable when one remembers that natural law is uniform and continuous. These recent discoveries go to swell the already large list of modern scientific ideas which correspond with the centuries-old Yogi teachings. When the Occult explanation that there is Life in everything, *inorganic as well as organic,* and that evolution is constant, is heard, then may we see that these experiments simply prove that the forms of life may be changed and developed—not that Life may be "created."

The chemical and mineral world furnish us with many instances of the growth and development of forms closely resembling the forms of the vegetable world. What is known as "metallic vegetation," as shown in the "lead tree," gives us an interesting example of this phenomenon. The experiment is performed by placing in a wide-necked bottle a clear acidulated solution of acetate of lead. The bottle is corked, a piece of copper wire being fastened to the cork, from which wire is suspended a piece of zinc, the latter hanging as nearly as possible in the center of the lead solution. When the bottle is corked the copper wire immediately begins to surround itself with a growth of metallic lead resembling fine moss. From this moss spring branches and limbs, which in turn manifest a growth similar to foliage, until at last a miniature bush or tree is formed. Similar "metallic vegetation" may be produced by other metallic solutions.

All of you have noticed how crystals of frost form on window panes in shapes of leaves, branches, foliage, flowers, blossoms, etc. Saltpeter when subjected to the effect of polarized light assumes forms closely resembling the forms of the orchid. Nature is full of these resemblances.

A German scientist recently performed a remarkable experiment with certain metallic salts. He subjected the salts to the action of a galvanic current, when to his surprise the particles of the salts grouped themselves around the negative pole of the battery, and then grew into a shape closely resembling a miniature mushroom, with tiny stem and umbrella top. These metallic mushrooms at first presented a transparent appearance, but gradually developed color, the top of the umbrella being a bright red, with a faint rose shade on the under surface. The stems showed a pale straw color. This was most interesting, but the important fact of the experiment consists in the discovery that these mushrooms have fine veins or tubes running along the stems, through which the nourishment, or additional material for growth, is transported, so that the growth is actually from the inside, just as is the case with fungus life. To all intents and purposes, these inorganic metallic growths were low forms of vegetable life.

But the search for Life does not end with the forms of the mineral world as we know them. Science has separated the material forms into smaller forms, and again still smaller. And if there is Life in the form composed of countless particles, then must there be Life in the particles themselves. For Life cannot come from non-Life, and if there be not Life in the particles, the theory of Omnipresent Life must fail. So we must look beyond the form and shape of the mineral—must separate it into its constituent parts, and then examine the parts for indications of Life.

Science teaches us that all forms of matter are composed of minute particles called molecules. A molecule is the smallest particle of matter that is possible, unless the chemical atoms composing the matter fly apart and the matter be resolved into its original elements. For instance, let us take the familiar instance of a drop of water. Let us divide and subdivide the drop, until at last we get to the smallest possible particle of water. That smallest possible particle would be a "molecule" of water. We cannot subdivide this molecule without causing its atoms of hydrogen and oxygen to fly apart—and then there would be no *water* at all. Well, these molecules manifest a something called Attraction for each other. They attract other molecules of the same kind, and are likewise attracted. The operation of this law of attraction results in the formation of masses of matter, whether those masses be mountains of solid rock, or a drop of water, or a volume of gas. All masses of matter are composed of aggregations of molecules, held together by the law of attraction. This law of attraction is called Cohesion. This Cohesive Attraction is not a mere mechanical force, as many suppose, but is an exhibition of Life action, manifesting in the presence of the molecule of a "like" or "love" for the similar molecule. And when the Life energies begin to manifest on a certain plane, and proceed to mould the molecules into crystals, so that we may see the actual process under way, we begin to realize very clearly that there is "something at work" in this building up.

But wonderful as this may seem to those unfamiliar with the idea, the manifestation of Life among the atoms is still more so. The atom, you will remember, is the chemical unit which, uniting with other atoms, makes up the molecule. For instance, if we take two atoms of the gas called hydrogen and one atom of the gas called oxygen, and place them near each other, they will at once rush toward each other and form a partnership, which is called a molecule of water. And so it is with all atoms—they are continually forming partnerships, or dissolving them. Marriage and divorce is a part of the life of the atoms. These evidences of attraction and repulsion among the atoms are receiving much attention from careful thinkers, and some of the most advanced minds of the age see in this phenomena the corroboration of the old Yogi idea that there is Life and vital action in the smallest particles of matter.

The atoms manifest vital characteristics in their attractions and repulsions. They move along the lines of their attractions and form marriages, and thus combining they form the substances with which we are familiar. When they combine, remember, they do not lose their individuality and melt into a permanent substance, but merely unite and yet remain distinct. If the combination be destroyed by chemical action, electrical discharge, etc., the atoms fly apart, and again live their own separate lives, until they come in contact with other atoms with which they have affinities, and form a new union or partnership. In many chemical changes the atoms divorce themselves, each forsaking its mate or mates, and seeking some newer affinity in the shape of a more congenial atom. The atoms manifest a fickleness and will always desert a lesser attraction for a greater one. This is no mere bit of imagery, or scientific poetry. It is a scientific statement of the action of atoms along the lines of vital manifestation.

The great German scientist, Haekel, has said: "I cannot imagine the simplest chemical and physical processes without attributing the movement of the material particles to unconscious sensation. The idea of Chemical Affinity consists in the fact that the various chemical elements perceive differences in the qualities of other elements, and experience pleasure or revulsion at contact with them, and execute their respective movements on this ground." He also says: "We may ascribe the feeling of pleasure or pain (satisfaction or dissatisfaction) to all atoms, and thereby ascribe the elective affinities of chemistry to the attraction between living atoms and repulsion between hating atoms." He also says that "the sensations in animal and plant life are connected by a long series of evolutionary stages with the simpler forms of sensation that we find in the inorganic elements, and that reveal themselves in chemical affinity." Naegli says: "If the molecules possess something that is related, however distantly, to sensation, it must be comfortable for them to be able to follow their attractions and repulsions, and uncomfortable for them when they are forced to do otherwise."

We might fill page after page with quotations from eminent thinkers going to prove the correctness of the old Yogi teachings that Life is Omnipresent. Modern Science is rapidly advancing to this position, leaving behind her the old idea of "dead matter." Even the new theories of the electron—the little particles of electrical energy which are now believed to constitute the base of the atom—does not change this idea, for the electrons manifest attraction, and response thereto, and form themselves into groups composing the atom. And even if we pass beyond matter into the mystical Ether which Science assumes to be the material base of things, we must believe that there is life there too, and that as Prof. Dolbear says: "The Ether has besides the function of energy and motion, other inherent properties, out of which could emerge, under proper circumstances, other phenomena, such as life, mind, or whatever may be in the substratum," and, that as Prof. Cope has hinted, that the basis of Life lies back of the atoms and may be found in the Universal Ether.

Some scientists go even further, and assert that not only is Life present in everything, but that Mind is present where Life is. Verily, the dreams of the Yogi fathers are coming true, and from the ranks of the materialists are coming the material proofs of the spiritual teachings. Listen to these words from Dr. Saleeby, in his recent valuable scientific work, "*Evolution, the Master Key.*" He says:

"Life is potential in matter; life-energy is not a thing unique and created at a particular time in the past. If evolution be true, living matter has been evolved by natural processes from matter which is, apparently, not alive. But if life is potential in matter, it is a thousand times more evident that Mind is potential in Life. The evolutionist is impelled to believe that Mind is potential in matter. (I adopt that form of words for the moment, but not without future criticism.) The microscopic cell, a minute speck of matter that is to become man, has in it the promise and the germ of mind. May we not then draw the inference that the elements of mind are present in those chemical elements—carbon, oxygen, hydrogen, nitrogen, sulphur, phosphorus, sodium, potassium, chlorine—that are found in the cell. Not only must we do so, but we must go further, since we know that each of these elements, and every other, is built up out of one invariable unit, the electron, and we must therefore assert that Mind is potential in the unit of Matter—the electron itself. * * * It is to assert the sublime truth first perceived by Spinoza, that Mind and Matter are the warp and woof of what Goethe called 'the living garment of God.' Both are complementary expressions of the Unknowable Reality which underlies both."

There is no such thing as non-vital attraction or repulsion. All inclinations for or against another object, or thing, is an evidence of Life. Each thing has sufficient life energy to enable it to carry on its work. And as each form advances by evolution into a higher form, it is able to have more of the Life energy manifest through it. As its material machinery is built up, it becomes able to manifest a greater and higher degree of Life. It is not that one thing has a low life, or another a high life—this cannot be, for there is but One Life. It is like the current of electricity that is able to run the most delicate machinery or manifest a light in the incandescent lamp. Give it the organ or machinery of manifestation, and it manifests—give it a low form, and it will manifest a low degree—give it a high form, and it will manifest a high degree. The same steam power runs the clumsy engine, or the perfect apparatus which drives the most delicate mechanism. And so it is with the One Life—its manifestations may seem low and clumsy, or high and perfect—but it all depends upon the material or mental machinery through which it works. There is but One Life, manifesting in countless forms and shapes, and degrees. One Life underlying All—in All.

From the highest forms of Life down through the animal, vegetable and mineral kingdoms, we see Life everywhere present—Death an illusion. Back of all visible forms of material life there is still the beginnings of manifested life pressing forward for expression and manifestation. And underneath all is the Spirit of Life—longing, striving, feeling, acting.

In the mountain and the ocean—the flower and the tree—the sunset—the dawn—the suns—the stars—all is Life—manifestations of the One Life. Everything is Alive, quick with living force, power, action; thrilling with vitality; throbbing with feeling; filled with activity. All is from the One Life—and all that is from the One Life is Alive. There is no dead substance in the Universe—there can be none—for Life cannot Die. All is Alive. And Life is in All.

Carry with you this Central Thought of the Lesson:

CENTRAL THOUGHT: *There is but One Life, and its manifestations comprise all the forms and shapes of the Universe. From Life comes but Life—and Life can come only from Life. Therefore we have the right to expect that all manifestations of the One Life should be Alive. And we are not mocked in such belief. Not only do the highest Occult Teachings inform us that Everything is Alive, but Modern Science has proven to us that Life is present everywhere—even in that which was formerly considered dead matter. It now sees that even the atom, and what lies back of the atom, is charged with Life Energy and Action. Forms and shapes may change, and do change—but Life remains eternal and infinite. It cannot Die—for it is LIFE.*

Peace be with thee.

THE THIRD LESSON

The Creative Will.

In our first lesson of this series, we stated that among the other qualities and attributes that we were compelled, by the laws of our reason, to think that the Absolute possessed, was that of Omnipotence or All-Power. In other words we are compelled to think of the One as being the source and fount of all the Power there is, ever has been, or ever can be in the Universe. Not only, as is generally supposed, that the Power of the One is greater than any other Power,—but more than this, that there can be no other power, and that, therefore, each and every, any and all manifestations or forms of Power, Force or Energy must be a part of the great one Energy which emanates from the One.

There is no escape from this conclusion, as startling as it may appear to the mind unaccustomed to it. If there is any power not from and of the One, from whence comes such power, for there is nothing else outside of the One? Who or what exists outside of the One that can manifest even the faintest degree of power of any kind? All power must come from the Absolute, and must in its nature be but one.

Modern Science has recognized this truth, and one of its fundamental principles is the Unity of Energy—the theory that all forms of Energy are, at the last, One. Science holds that all forms of Energy are interchangeable, and from this idea comes the theory of the Conservation of Energy or Corelation of Force.

Science teaches that every manifestation of energy, power, or force, from the operation of the law of gravitation, up to the highest form of mental force is but the operation of the One Energy of the Universe.

Just what this Energy is, in its inner nature, Science does not know. It has many theories, but does not advance any of them as a law. It speaks of the Infinite and Eternal Energy from which all things proceed, but pronounces its nature to be unknowable. But some of the latter-day scientists are veering around to the teachings of the occultists, and are now hinting that it is something more than a mere mechanical energy. They are speaking of it in terms of mind. Wundt, the German scientist, whose school of thought is called voluntarism, considers the motive-force of Energy to be something that may be called Will. Crusius, as far back as 1744 said: "Will is the dominating force of the world." And Schopenhauer based his fascinating but gloomy philosophy and metaphysics upon the underlying principle of an active form of energy which he called the Will-to-Live, which he considered to be the Thing-in-Itself, or the Absolute. Balzac, the novelist, considered a something akin to Will, to be the moving force of the Universe. Bulwer advanced a similar theory, and made mention of it in several of his novels.

This idea of an active, creative Will, at work in the Universe, building up; tearing down; replacing; repairing; changing—always at work—ever active—has been entertained by numerous philosophers and thinkers, under different names and styles. Some, like Schopenhauer have thought of this *Will* as the final thing—that which took the place of God—the First Cause. But others have seen in this Will an active living principle emanating from the Absolute or God, and working in accordance with the laws impressed by Him upon it. In various forms, this latter idea is seen all through the history of philosophical thought. Cudsworth, the English philosopher, evolved the idea of a something called the "Plastic Nature," which so closely approaches the Yogi idea of the Creative Will, that we feel justified in quoting a passage from his book. He says:

"It seems not so agreeable to reason that Nature, as a distinct thing from the Deity, should be quite superseded or made to signify nothing, God Himself doing all things immediately and miraculously; from whence it would follow also that they are all done either forcibly and violently, or else artificially only, and none of them by any inward principle of their own.

"This opinion is further confuted by that slow and gradual process that in the generation of things, which would seem to be but a vain and idle pomp or a trifling formality if the moving power were omnipotent; as also by those errors and bungles which are committed where the matter is inept and contumacious; which argue that the moving power be not irresistible, and that Nature is such a thing as is not altogether incapable (as well as human art) of being sometimes frustrated and disappointed by the indisposition of matter. Whereas an omnipotent moving power, as it could dispatch its work in a moment, so would it always do it infallibly and irresistibly, no ineptitude and stubbornness of matter being ever able to hinder such a one, or make him bungle or fumble in anything.

"Wherefore, since neither all things are produced fortuitously, or by the unguided mechanism of matter, nor God himself may be reasonably thought to do all things immediately and miraculously, it may well be concluded that there is a Plastic Nature under him, which, as an inferior and subordinate instrument, doth drudgingly execute that part of his providence which consists in the regular and orderly motion of matter; yet so as there is also besides this a higher providence to be acknowledged, which, presiding over it, doth often supply the defects of it, and sometimes overrules it, forasmuch as the Plastic Nature cannot act electively nor with discretion."

The Yogi Philosophy teaches of the existence of a Universal Creative Will, emanating from the Absolute—infilled with the power of the Absolute and acting under established natural laws, which performs the active work of creation in the world, similar to that performed by "Cudsworth's Plastic Nature," just mentioned. This Creative Will is not Schopenhauer's Will-to-Live. It is not a Thing-in-itself, but a vehicle or instrument of the Absolute. It is an emanation of the mind of the Absolute—a manifestation in action of its Will—a mental product rather than a physical, and, of course, saturated with the life-energy of its projector.

This Creative Will is not a mere blind, mechanical energy or force—it is far more than this. We can explain it only by referring you to the manifestation of the Will in yourself. You wish to move your arm, and it moves. The immediate force may seem to be a mechanical force, but what is back of that force—what is the essence of the force? The Will! All manifestations of energy—all the causes of motion—all forces—are forms of the action of the Will of the One—the Creative Will—acting under natural laws established by the One, ever moving, acting, forcing, urging, driving, leading. We do not mean that every little act is a thought of the moment on the part of the Absolute, and a reaching out of the Will in obedience to that thought. On the contrary, we mean that the One set the Will into operation as a whole, conceiving of laws and limitations in its action, the Will constantly operating in obedience to that conception, the results manifesting in what we call natural law; natural forces, etc. Besides this, the Absolute is believed to manifest its Will specially upon occasions; and moreover permits its Will to be applied and used by the individual wills of individual Egos, under the general Law and laws, and plan of the One.

But you must not suppose that the Will is manifested only in the form of mechanical forces, cohesion, chemical attraction, electricity, gravitation, etc.

It does more than this. It is in full operation in all forms of life, and living things. It is present everywhere. Back of all forms of movement and action, we find a moving cause—usually a *Pressure*. This is true of that which we have been calling mechanical forces, and of all forms of that which we call Life Energy. Now, note this, this great Pressure that you will observe in all Life Action, is the Creative Will—the Will Principle of the One—bending toward the carrying out of the Great Plan of Life.

Look where we will, on living forms, and we may begin to recognize the presence of a certain creative energy at work—building up; moulding, directing; tearing down; replacing, etc.—always active in its efforts to create, preserve and conserve life. This visible creative energy is what the Yogi Philosophy calls "the Creative Will," and which forms the subject of this lesson. The Creative Will is that striving, longing, pressing forward, unfolding, progressing evolutionary effort, that all thoughtful people see in operation in all forms of life—throughout all Nature. From the lowest to the highest forms of life, the Effort, Energy, Pressure, may be recognized in action, creating, preserving, nourishing, and improving its forms. It is that Something that we recognize when we speak of "Nature's Forces" at work in plant growth and animal functioning. If you will but keep the word and idea—"NATURE"—before you, you will be able to more clearly form the mental concept of the Creative Will. The Creative Will is that which you have been calling "Nature at Work" in the growth of the plant; the sprouting of the seed; the curling and reaching of the tendril; the fertilization of the blossoms, etc. You have seen this Will at work, if you have watched growing things.

We call this energy "the Creative Will," because it is the objective manifestation of the Creative Energy of the Absolute—Its visible Will manifested in the direction of physical life. It is as much Will in action, as the Will that causes your arm to move in response to its power. It is no mere chance thing, or mechanical law—it is life action in operation.

This Creative Will not only causes movement in completed life, but all movement and action in life independent of the personal will of its individual forms. All the phenomena of the so-called Unconscious belong to it. It causes the body to grow; attends to the details of nourishment, assimilation, digestion, elimination, and all of the rest. It builds up bodies, organs, and parts, and keeps them in operation and function.

The Creative Will is directed to the outward expression of Life—to the objectification of Life. You may call this energy the "Universal Life Energy" if you wish, but, to those who know it, it is a Will—an active, living Will, in full operation and power, pressing forward toward the manifestation of objective life.

The Creative Will seems to be filled with a strong Desire to manifest. It longs to express itself, and to give birth to forms of activity. Desire lies under and in all forms of its manifestations. The ever present

Desire of the Creative Will causes lower forms to be succeeded by higher forms—and is the moving cause of evolution—it is the Evolutionary Urge itself, which ever cries to its manifestations, "Move on; move upward."

In the Hindu classic, the "Mahabarata," Brahma created the most beautiful female being ever known, and called her Tillotama. He presented her in turn to all the gods, in order to witness their wonder and admiration. Siva's desire to behold her was so great that it developed in him four faces, in succession, as she made the tour of the assembly; and Indra's longing was so intense that his body became all eyes. In this myth may be seen exemplified the effect of Desire and Will in the forms of life, function and shape —all following Desire and Need, as in the case of the long neck of the giraffe which enables him to reach for the high branches of the trees in his native land; and in the long neck and high legs of the fisher birds, the crane, stork, ibis, etc.

The Creative Will finds within itself a desire to create suns, and they are formed. It desired planets to revolve around the suns, and they were thrown off in obedience to the law. It desired plant life, and plant life appeared, working from higher to lower form. Then came animal life, from nomad to man. Some of the animal forms yielded to the desire to fly, and wings appeared gradually, and we called it bird-life. Some felt a desire to burrow in the ground, and lo! came the moles, gophers, etc. It wanted a thinking creature, and Man with his wonderful brain was evolved. Evolution is more than a mere survival of the fittest; natural selection, etc. Although it uses these laws as tools and instruments, still back of them is that insistent urge—that ever-impelling desire—that ever-active Creative Will. Lamark was nearer right than Darwin when he claimed that Desire was back of it all, and preceded function and form. Desire wanted form and function, and produced them by the activity of the Creative Will.

This Creative Will acts like a living force—and so it is indeed—but it does not act as a reasoning, intellectual Something, in one sense—instead it manifests rather the "feeling," wanting, longing, instinctive phase of mind, akin to those "feelings" and resulting actions that we find within our natures. The Will acts on the Instinctive Plane.

Evolution shows us Life constantly pressing forward toward higher and still higher forms of expression. The urge is constantly upward and onward. It is true that some species sink out of sight, their work in the world having been done, but they are succeeded by other species more in harmony with their environment and the needs of their times. Some races of men decay, but others build on their foundations, and reach still greater heights.

The Creative Will is something different from Reason or Intellect. But it underlies these. In the lower forms of life, in which mind is in but small evidence, the Will is in active operation, manifesting in Instinct and Automatic Life Action, so called. It does not depend upon brains for manifestation—for these lowly forms of life have no brains—but is in operation through every part of the body of the living thing.

Evidences of the existence of the Creative Will acting independently of the brains of animal and plant life may be had in overwhelming quantity if we will but examine the life action in the lower forms of life.

The testimony of the investigators along the lines of the Evolutionary school of thought, show us that the Life Principle was in active operation in lowly animal and plant life millions of years before brains capable of manifesting Thought were produced. Haekel informs us that during more than half of the enormous time that has elapsed since organic life first became evident, no animal sufficiently advanced to have a brain was in existence. Brains were evolved according to the law of desire or necessity, in accordance with the Great Plan, but they were not needed for carrying on the wonderful work of the creation and preservation of the living forms. And they are not today. The tiny infant, and the senseless idiot are not able to think intelligently, but still their life functions go on regularly and according to law, in spite of the absence of thinking brains. And the life work of the plants, and of the lowly forms of animal life, is carried on likewise. This wonderful thing that we call Instinct is but another name for the manifestation of the Creative Will which flows from the One Life, or the Absolute.

Even as far down the scale of life as the Monera, we may see the Creative Will in action. The Monera are but tiny bits of slimy, jelly-like substances—mere specks of glue without organs of any kind, and yet they exercise the organic phenomena of life, such as nutrition, reproduction, sensation and movement, all of which are usually associated with an organized structure. These creatures are incapable of thought in themselves, and the phenomenon is due to the action of the Will through them. This Instinctive impulse and action is seen everywhere, manifesting upon higher and still higher lines, as higher forms of organisms are built up.

Scientists have used the term, "Appetency," defining it as, "the instinctive tendency of living organisms to perform certain actions; the tendency of an unorganized body to seek that which satisfies the wants of its organism." Now what is this tendency? It cannot be an effort of reason, for the low form of life has nothing with which to reason. And it is impossible to think of "purposive tendency" without assuming the existence of mental power of some kind. And where can such a power be located if not in the form itself? When we consider that the Will is acting in and through all forms of Life, from highest to lowest—from Moneron to Man—we can at once recognize the source of the power and activity. It is the Great Life Principle—the Creative Will, manifesting itself.

We can perhaps better form an idea of the Creative

Will, by reference to its outward and visible forms of activity. We cannot see the Will itself—the Pressure and the Urge—but we can see its action through living forms. Just as we cannot see a man behind a curtain, and yet may practically see him by watching the movements of his form as he presses up against the curtain, so may we see the Will by watching it as it presses up against the living curtain of the forms of life. There was a play presented on the American stage a few years ago, in which one of the scenes pictured the place of departed spirits according to the Japanese belief. The audience could not see the actors representing the spirits, but they could see their movements as they pressed up close to a thin silky curtain stretched across the stage, and their motions as they moved to and fro behind the curtain were plainly recognized. The deception was perfect, and the effect was startling. One almost believed that he saw the forms of formless creatures. And this is what we may do in viewing the operation of the Creative Will—we may take a look at the moving form of the Will behind the curtain of the forms of the manifestation of life. We may see it pressing and urging here, and bending there—building up here, and changing there—always acting, always moving, striving, doing, in response to that insatiable urge and craving, and longing of its inner desire. Let us take a few peeps at the Will moving behind the curtain!

Commencing with the cases of the forming of the

crystals, as spoken of in our last lesson, we may pass on to plant life. But before doing so, it may be well for us to take a parting look at the Will manifesting crystal forms. One of the latest scientific works makes mention of the experiments of a scientist who has been devoting much attention to the formation of crystals, and reports that he has noticed that certain crystals of organic compounds, instead of being built up symmetrically, as is usual with crystals, were "enantion-morphic," that is, opposed to each other, in rights and lefts, like hands or gloves, or shoes, etc. These crystals are never found alone, but always form in pairs. Can you not see the Will behind the curtain here?

Let us look for the Will in plant-life. Passing rapidly over the wonderful evidences in the cases of the fertilization of plants by insects, the plant shaping its blossom so as to admit the entrance of the particular insect that acts as the carrier of its pollen, think for a moment how the distribution of the seed is provided for. Fruit trees and plants surround the seed with a sweet covering, that it may be eaten by insect and animal, and the seed distributed. Others have a hard covering to protect the seed or nut from the winter frosts, but which covering rots with the spring rains and allows the germ to sprout. Others surround the seed with a fleecy substance, so that the wind may carry it here and there and give it a chance to find a home where it is not so crowded. Another tree has a little pop-gun arrangement, by means of which it pops its seed to a distance of several feet.

Other plants have seeds that are covered with a burr or "sticky" bristles, which enables them to attach themselves to the wool of sheep and other animals, and thus be carried about and finally dropped in some spot far away from the parent plant, and thus the scattering of the species be accomplished. Some plants show the most wonderful plans and arrangements for this scattering of the seed in new homes where there is a better opportunity for growth and development, the arrangements for this purpose displaying something very much akin to what we would call "ingenuity" if it were the work of a reasoning mind. There are plants called cockle-burs whose seed-pods are provided with stickers in every direction, so that anything brushing against them is sure to pick them up. At the end of each sticker is a very tiny hook, and these hooks fasten themselves tightly into anything that brushes against it, animal wool, hair, or clothing, etc. Some of these seeds have been known to have been carried to other quarters of the globe in wool, etc., there to find new homes and a wider field.

Other plants, like the thistle, provide their seed with downy wings, by which the wind carries them afar to other fields. Other seeds have a faculty of tumbling and rolling along the ground to great distances, owing to their peculiar shape and formation. The maple provides its seed with a peculiar arrangement something like a propeller screw, which when the wind strikes the trees and looses the seed, whirls the latter through the air to a distance of a hundred yards or more. Other seeds are provided with floating apparatus, which enables them to travel many miles by stream or river, or rain washes. Some of these not only float, but actually swim, having spider-like filaments, which wriggle like legs, and actually propel the tiny seed along to its new home. A recent writer says of these seeds that "so curiously lifelike are their movements that it is almost impossible to believe that these tiny objects, making good progress through the water, are really seeds, and not insects."

The leaves of the Venus' Fly-trap fold upon each other and enclose the insect which is attracted by the sweet juice on the leaf, three extremely sensitive bristles or hairs giving the plant notice that the insect is touching them. A recent writer gives the following description of a peculiar plant. He says: "On the shores of Lake Nicaragua is to be found an uncanny product of the vegetable kingdom known among the natives by the expressive name of 'the Devil's Noose.' Dunstan, the naturalist, discovered it long ago while wandering on the shores of the lake. Attracted by the cries of pain and terror from his dog, he found the animal held by black sticky bands which had chafed the skin to bleeding point. These bands were branches of a newly-discovered carnivorous plant which had been aptly named the 'land octopus.' The branches are flexible, black, polished and without leaves, and secrete a viscid fluid."

You have seen flowers that closed when you touched them. You remember the Golden Poppy that closes when the sun goes down. Another plant, a variety of orchid, has a long, slender, flat stem, or tube, about one-eighth of an inch thick, with an opening at the extreme end, and a series of fine tubes where it joins the plant. Ordinarily this tube remains coiled up into a spiral, but when the plant needs water (it usually grows upon the trunks of trees overhanging swampy places) it slowly uncoils the little tube and bends it over until it dips into the water, when it proceeds to suck up the water until it is filled, when it slowly coils around and discharges the water directly upon the plant, or its roots. Then it repeats the process until the plant is satisfied. When the water is absent from under the plant the tube moves this way and that way until it finds what it wants—just like the trunk of an elephant. If one touches the tube or trunk of the plant while it is extended for water, it shows a great sensitiveness and rapidly coils itself up. Now what causes this life action? The plant has no brains, and cannot have reasoned out this process, nor even have acted upon them by reasoning processes. It has nothing to think with to such a high degree. It is the Will behind the curtain, moving this way and that way, and doing things.

There was once a French scientist named Duhamel. He planted some beans in a cylinder—something like a long tomato can lying on its side. He waited until the beans began to sprout, and send forth roots downward, and shoots upward, according to nature's invariable rule. Then he moved the cylinder a little—

rolled it over an inch or two. The next day he rolled it over a little more. And so on each day, rolling it over a little each time. Well, after a time Duhamel shook the dirt and growing beans out of the cylinder, and what did he find? This, that the beans in their endeavor to grow their roots downward had kept on bending each day downward; and in their endeavor to send shoots upward, had kept on bending upward a little each day, until at last there had been formed two complete spirals—the one spiral being the roots ever turning downward, and the other the shoots ever bending upward. How did the plant know direction? What was the moving power. The Creative Will behind the curtain again, you see!

Potatoes in dark cellars have sent out roots or sprouts twenty and thirty feet to reach light. Plants will send out roots many feet to reach water. They know where the water and light are, and where to reach them. The tendrils of a plant know where the stake or cord is, and they reach out for it and twine themselves around it. Unwind them, and the next day they are found again twined around it. Move the stake or cord, and the tendril moves after it. The insect-eating plants are able to distinguish between nitrogenous and non-nitrogenous food, accepting the one and rejecting the other. They recognize that cheese has the same nourishing properties as the insect, and they accept it, although it is far different in feeling, taste, appearance and every other characteristic from their accustomed food.

Case after case might be mentioned and cited to show the operation of the Will in plant-life. But wonderful as are many of these cases, the mere action of the Will as shown in the *growing* of the plant is just as wonderful. Just imagine a tiny seed, and see it sprout and draw to itself the nourishment from water, air, light and soil, then upward until it becomes a great tree with bark, limbs, branches, leaves, blossoms, fruit and all. Think of this miracle, and consider what must be the power and nature of that Will that causes it.

The growing plant manifests sufficient strength to crack great stones, and lift great slabs of pavement, as may be noticed by examining the sidewalks of suburban towns and parks. An English paper prints a report of four enormous mushrooms having lifted a huge slab of paving stone in a crowded street overnight. Think of this exhibition of Energy and Power. This wonderful faculty of exerting force and motion and energy is fundamental in the Will, for indeed every physical change and growth is the result of motion, and motion arises only from force and pressure. Whose force, energy, power and motion? The Will's!

On all sides of us we may see this constant and steady urge and pressure behind living forces, and inorganic forms as well—always a manifestation of Energy and Power. And all this Power is in the Will—and the Will is but the manifestation of the All-Power—the Absolute. Remember this.

And this power manifests itself not only in the

matter of growth and ordinary movements, but also in some other ways that seem quite mysterious to even modern Science. How is it that certain birds are able to fly directly against a strong wind, without visible movement of their wings? How do the buzzards float in the air, and make speed without a motion of the wing? What is the explanation of the movements of certain microscopic creatures who lack organs of movement? Listen to this instance related by the scientist Benet. He states that the Polycystids have a most peculiar manner of moving—a sort of sliding motion, to the right or left, upward, backward, sideways, stopping and starting, fast or slow, as it wills. It has no locomotive organs, and no movement can be seen to take place in the body from within or without. It simply slides. How?

Passing on to the higher animal life—how do eggs grow into chickens? What is the power in the germ of the egg? Can the germ think, and plan, and move, and grow into a chicken? Or is the Will at work there? And what is true in this case, is true of the birth and growth of all animal life—all animal life develops from a single germ cell. How, and Why?

There is a mental energy resident in the germ cell—of this there can be no doubt. And that mental energy is the Creative Will ever manifesting. Listen to these words from Huxley, the eminent scientist. He says:

"The student of Nature wonders the more and is astonished the less, the more conversant he becomes with her operations; but of all the perennial miracles she offers to his inspection, perhaps the most worthy of his admiration is the development of a plant or of an animal from its embryo. Examine the recently laid egg of some common animal, such as a salamander or a newt. It is a minute spheroid in which the best microscope will reveal nothing but a structureless sac, enclosing a glairy fluid, holding granules in suspension. But strange possibilities lie dormant in that semi-fluid globule. Let a moderate supply of warmth reach its watery cradle, and the plastic matter undergoes changes so rapid, and so purposelike in their succession, that one can only compare them to those operated by a skilled modeller upon a formless lump of clay. As with an invisible trowel, the mass is divided and subdivided into smaller and smaller portions, until it is reduced to an aggregation of granules not too large to build withal the finest fabrics of the nascent organism. And, then, it is as if a delicate finger traced out the line to be occupied by the spinal column, and moulded the contour of the body; pinching up the head at one end, the tail at the other, and fashioning flank and limb into due salamanderine proportions, in so artistic a way that, after watching the process hour by hour, one is almost involuntarily possessed by the notion that some more subtle aid to vision than the achromatic lens would show the hidden artist, with his plan before him, striving with skilful manipulation to perfect his work.

"As life advances and the young amphibian ranges the waters, the terror of his insect contemporaries, not only are the nutritious particles supplied by its prey (by the addition of which to its frame growth takes place) laid down, each in its proper spot, and in due proportion to the rest, as to reproduce the form, the color, and the size, characteristic of the parental stock; but even the wonderful powers of reproducing lost parts possessed by these animals are controlled by the same governing tendency. Cut off the legs, the tail, the jaws, separately or all together, and as Spallanzani showed long ago, these parts not only grow again, but the new limb is formed on the same type as those which were lost. The new jaw, or leg, is a newt's, and never by any accident more like that of a frog's."

In this passage from Huxley one may see the actual working of the Creative Will of the Universe,—moving behind the curtain—and a very thin curtain at that. And this wonderful work is going on all around us, all the time. Miracles are being accomplished every second—they are so common that we fail to regard them.

And in our bodies is the Will at work? Most certainly. What built you up from single cell to maturity? Did you do it with your intellect? Has not every bit of it been done without your conscious knowledge? It is only when things go wrong, owing to the violation of some law, that you become aware of your internal organs. And, yet, stomach and liver, and heart and the rest have been performing their work steadily—working away day and night, building up, repairing, nourishing, growing you into a man or woman, and keeping you sound and strong. Are you doing this with your reason or with your personal will? No, it is the great Creative Will of the Universe,—the expression of the purpose and power of the One, working in and through you. It is the One Life manifesting in you through its Creative Will.

And not only is this all. The Creative Will is all around us in every force, energy and principle. The force that we call mental power is the principle of the Will directed by our individual minds. In this statement we have a hint of the great mystery of Mental Force and Power, and the so-called Psychic Phenomena. It also gives us a key to Mental Healing. This is not the place to go into detail regarding these phases—but think over it a bit. This Will Power of the Universe, in all of its forms and phases, from Electricity to Thought-power, is always at the disposal of Man, within limits, and subject always to the laws of the Creative Will of the Universe. Those who acquire an understanding of the laws of any force may use it. And any force may be used or misused.

And the nearer in understanding and consciousness that we get to the One Life and Power, the greater will be our possible power, for we are thus getting closer and closer to the source of All Power. In these lessons we hope to be able to tell you how you may come into closer touch with this One Life of which you and all living things are but forms, shapes and channels of expression, under the operation of the Creative Will.

We trust that this lesson may have brought to your minds the realization of the Oneness of All—the fact that we are all parts of the one encircling unity, the heart-throbs and pulsations of which are to be felt even to the outer edge of the circle of life—in Man, in Monad, in Crystal, in Atom. Try to feel that inner essence of Creative Will that is within yourselves, and endeavor to realize your complete inner unity in it, with all other forms of life. Try to realize, as some recent writer has expressed it, "that all the living world is but mankind in the making, and that we are but part of the All." And also remember that splendid vistas of future unfoldment spread themselves out before the gaze of the awakened soul, until the mind fails to grasp the wondrous sight.

We will now close this lesson by calling your attention to its

CENTRAL THOUGHT.

There is but One Power in the Universe—One Energy—One Force. And that Power, Energy and Force is a manifestation of the One Life. There can be no other Power, for there is none other than the One from whom Power may come. And there can be no manifestation of Power that is not the Power of the One, for no other Power can be in existence. The Power of the One is visible in its manifestations to us in the natural laws and forces of Nature—which we call the Creative Will. This Creative Will is the inner moving power, urge and pressure behind all forms and shapes of Life. In atom, and molecule; in monad, in cell, in plant, in fish, in animal, in man,—the Life Principle or Creative Will is constantly in action, creating, preserving, and carrying on life in its functions. We may call this Instinct or Nature, but it is the Creative Will in action. This Will is back of all Power, Energy, or Force—be it physical, mechanical or mental force. And all Force that we use, consciously or unconsciously, comes from the One Great Source of Power. If we could but see clearly, we would know that back of us is the Power of the Universe, awaiting our intelligent uses, under the control of the Will of the All. There is nothing to be afraid of, for we are manifestations of the One Life, from which all Power proceeds, and the Real Self is above the effect, for it is part of the Cause. But over and above—under and behind—all forms of Being, Matter, Energy, Force and Power, is the ABSOLUTE—ever Calm; ever Peaceful; ever Content. In knowing this it becomes us to manifest that spirit of absolute Trust, Faith and Confidence in the Goodness and Ultimate Justice of That which is the only Reality there is.

Peace be with you.

THE FOURTH LESSON

The Unity of Life.

In our First Lesson of this series we spoke of the One Reality underlying all Life. This One Reality was stated to be higher than mind or matter, the nearest term that can be applied to it being "Spirit." We told you that it was impossible to explain just what "Spirit" is, for we have nothing else with which to compare or describe it, and it can be expressed only in its own terms, and not in the terms applicable to its emanations or manifestations. But, as we said in our First Lesson, we may think of "Spirit" as meaning the "essence" of Life and Being—the Reality underlying Universal Life, and from which the latter emanates.

In the Second Lesson we stated that this "Spirit," which we called "The Absolute," expressed itself in the Universal Life, which Universal Life manifested itself in countless forms of life and activity. In the same lesson we showed you that the Universe is alive—that there is not a single dead thing in it—that there can be no such thing as a dead object in the Universe, else the theory and truth of the One underlying Life must fall and be rejected. In that lesson we also showed you that even in the world of inorganic things there was ever manifest life—in every atom and particle of inorganic matter there is the universal life energy manifesting itself, and in constant activity.

In the Third Lesson, we went still further into this phase of the general subject, and showed you that the Creative Will—that active principle of the Universal

Life—was ever at work, building up new forms, shapes and combinations, and then tearing them down for the purpose of rebuilding the material into new forms, shapes, and combinations. The Creative Will is ever at work in its threefold function of creating, preserving and destroying forms—the change, however, being merely in the shape and form or combination, the real substance remaining unchanged in its inner aspect, notwithstanding the countless apparent changes in its objective forms. Like the great ocean the depths of which remain calm and undisturbed, and the real nature of which is unchanged in spite of the waves, and billows of surface manifestation, so does the great ocean of the Universal Life remain unchanged and unaltered in spite of the constant play of the Creative Will upon the surface. In the same lesson we gave you many examples of the Will in action—of its wondrous workings in the various forms of life and activity—all of which went to show you that the One Power was at work everywhere and at all times.

In our next lesson—the Fifth Lesson—we shall endeavor to make plain to you the highest teachings of the Yogi Philosophy regarding the One Reality and the Many Manifestations—the One and the Many—how the One apparently becomes Many—that great question and problem which lies at the bottom of the well of truth. In that lesson we shall present for your consideration some fundamental and startling truths, but before we reach that point in our teachings, we must fasten upon your mind the basic truth that all the various manifestations of Life that we see on all hands in the Universe are but forms of manifestation of One Universal Life which is itself an emanation of the Absolute.

Speaking generally, we would say to you that the emanation of the Absolute is in the form of a grand manifestation of One Universal Life, in which the various apparent separate forms of Life are but centers of Energy or Consciousness, the separation being more apparent than real, there being a bond of unity and connection underlying all the apparently separated forms. Unless the student gets this idea firmly fixed in his mind and consciousness, he will find it difficult to grasp the higher truths of the Yogi Philosophy. That all Life is One, at the last,—that all forms of manifestation of Life are in harmonious Unity, underlying—is one of the great basic truths of the Yogi Teaching, and all the students of that philosophy must make this basic truth their own before they may progress further. This grasping of the truth is more than a mere matter of intellectual conception, for the intellect reports that all forms of Life are separate and distinct from each other, and that there can be no unity amidst such diversity. But from the higher parts of the mind comes the message of an underlying Unity, in spite of all apparent diversity, and if one will meditate upon this idea he will soon begin to realize the truth, and will *feel* that he, himself, is but a center of consciousness in a great ocean of Life—that he and all other centers are connected by countless spiritual and mental filaments—and that all emerge from the One. He will find that the illusion of separateness is but "a working fiction of the Universe," as one writer has so aptly described it—and that All is One, at the last, and underlying all is One.

Some of our students may feel that we are taking too long a path to lead up to the great basic truths of our philosophy, but we who have traveled The Path, and know its rocky places and its sharp turns, feel justified in insisting that the student be led to the truth gradually and surely, instead of attempting to make short cuts across dangerous ravines and canyons. We must insist upon presenting our teachings in our own way—for this way has been tested and found good. We know that every student will come to realize that our plan is a wise one, and that he will thank us for giving him this gradual and easy approach to the wondrous and awful truth which is before us. By this gradual process, the mind becomes accustomed to the line of thought and the underlying principles, and also gradually discards wornout mental sheaths which have served their purposes, and which must be discarded because they begin to weigh heavily upon the mind as it reaches the higher altitudes of The Path of Attainment. Therefore, we must ask you to consider with us, in this lesson, some further teachings regarding the Unity of Life.

All the schools of the higher Oriental thought, as well as many of the great philosophical minds of the Western world, have agreed upon the conception of the Unity of Life—the Oneness of All Life. The Western thinkers, and many of the Eastern philosophers arrived at this conclusion by means of their Intellectual powers, greatly heightened and stimulated by concentration and meditation, which latter process liberated the faculties of the Spiritual Mind so that it passed down knowledge to the Intellect, which then seized upon the higher knowledge which it found within itself, and amplified and theorized upon the same. But among the Eastern Masters there are other sources of information open, and from these sources come the same report—the Oneness and Unity of Universal Life. These higher sources of information to which we have alluded, consist of the knowledge coming from those Beings who have passed on to higher planes of Life than ours, and whose awakened spiritual faculties and senses enable them to see things quite plainly which are quite dark to us. And from these sources, also, comes the message of the Oneness of Life—of the existence of a wonderful Universal Life including all forms of life as we know it, and many forms and phases unknown to us—many centers in the great Ocean of Life. No matter how high the source of inquiry, the answer is the same—"All Life is One." And this One Life includes Beings as much higher than ourselves, as we are higher than the creatures in the slime of the ocean-bed. Included in it are beings who would seem as archangels or gods to us, and they inform us that beyond them are still higher and more radiant creatures, and so on to infinity of infinities. And yet all are but centers of Being in the One Life—all but a part of the great Universal Life, which itself is but an emanation of The Absolute.

The mind of man shrinks back appalled from the contemplation of such wonders, and yet there are men who dare to attempt to speak authoritatively of the attributes and qualities of "God," as if He, the Absolute, were but a magnified man. Verily, indeed, "fools rush in where angels fear to tread," as the poet hath said.

Those who will read our next lesson and thus gain an idea of the sublime conception of the Absolute held by the Yogi teachers may shudder at the presumption of those mortals who dare to think of the Absolute as possessing "attributes" and "qualities" like unto the meanest of things in this his emanated Universe. But even these spiritual infants are doing well—that is, they are beginning to *think,* and when man begins to *think* and *question,* he begins to progress. It is not the fact of these people's immature ideas that has caused these remarks on our part, but rather their tendency to set up their puny conceptions as the absolute truth, and then insisting upon forcing these views upon the outer world of men, whom they consider "poor ignorant heathen." Permit each man to think acording to his light—and help him by offering to share with him the best that you possess—but do not attempt to force upon him your own views as absolute truth to be swallowed by him under threat of damnation or eternal punishment. Who are you that dares to speak of punishment and damnation, when the smell of the smoke of the hell of materialism is still upon your robes. When you realize just what spiritual infants you still are—the best of you—you will blush at these things. Hold fast to the best that you know—be generous to others who seem to wish to share your knowledge—but give without blame or feeling of superiority—for those whom you teach to-day may be your teachers tomorrow—there are many surprises of this kind along The Path. Be brave and confident, but when you begin to feel puffed up by your acquirement of some new bit of knowledge, let your prayer—*our* prayer, for we too are infants—be, "Lord, be merciful unto me, a fool!"

The above words are for us, the students of the Yogi Philosophy—the teachers of the same—for human nature is the same in spite of names, and we must avoid the "vanity of vanities"—Spiritual Pride and Arrogance—that fault which has sent many a soul tumbling headlong from a high position on The Path, and compelled it to again begin the journey, chastened and bruised. The fall of Lucifer has many correspondences upon the occult plane, and is, indeed, in itself an allegorical illustration of just this law. Remember, always, that you are but a Centre in the Ocean of Life, and that all others are Centres in the same ocean, and that underlying both and all of you is the same calm bed of Life and Knowledge, the property of all. The highest and the lowest are part of the same One Life—each of you has the same life blood flowing through your veins—you are connected with every other form of life, high or low, with invisible bonds, and none is separate from another. We are speaking, of course, to the personalities of the various students who are reading these words. The Real Self of each is above the need of such advice and caution, and those who are able to reach the Real Self in consciousness have no need for these words, for they have outlived this stage of error.

To many, the consciousness of the One Life— the Universal Life—in which all are centres of consciousness and being—has come gradually as a final step of a long series of thought and reasoning, aided by flashes of truth from the higher regions of the mind. To others it has come as a great illumination, or flash of Truth, in which all things are seen in their proper relations and positions to each other, and all as phases of being in the One. The term "Cosmic Consciousness," which has been used in the previous series of these lessons, and by other writers, means this sudden flash of "knowing" in which all the illusionary dividing lines between persons and things are broken down and the Universal Life is seen to be actually existent as One Life. To those who have reached this consciousness by either route just mentioned—or by other routes—there is no sense of loss of individuality or power or strength. On the contrary there is always a new sense of increased power and strength and knowing —instead of losing Individuality, there is a sense of having found it. One feels that he has the whole Universe at his back, or within him, rather than that he has lost his identity in the great Ocean of Life.

While we are speaking of this phase of the subject, we should like to ask you if you have ever investigated and inquired into the real meaning of the much-used word "Individuality?" Have you ever looked up its origin and real meaning, as given by the standard authorities? We are sure that many of you have no real idea of the actual meaning of the term, as strange as this statement may appear to you at first glance. Stop now, and define the word to yourself, as you have been accustomed to think of it. Ninety-five people of a hundred will tell you that it means something like "a strong personality." Let us see about this.

Webster defines the word "Individual" as follows: "Not divided, or not to be divided; existing as one distinct being or object; single; one." The same authority informs us that the word arises from the Latin word *individuus,* meaning "indivisible; not divisible." Does not this help you to gain a clearer idea of the Individuality that knows itself to be a Centre of Consciousness in the One Life, rather than a separate, puny, insignificant thing apart from all other centres or forms of Life, or the source of Life? We think it will help to clear your mind of some of the fog that has not as yet lifted itself.

And while we are on the subject of definitions, let us take a little look at the word "Personality," that is generally believed to be a synonym of "Individuality," and is often so used. Webster tells us that the word "Person" originated from the Latin word *persona,* meaning "a mask used by actors," which word in turn arose from two other words, *per,* meaning "through," and *sonare,* meaning "to sound," the two combined words meaning "to sound through." The same authority informs us that the archaic meaning of the word was "a character or part, as in a play; an assumed character." If you will think of Personality as "a mask used by an actor," or as "a part in a play," or as something used to "sound through" or to speak through, by the real Individual behind the mask of Personality, then perhaps you will see a little further into the Mystery of Personality and Individuality.

Oh, dear students, be not deceived by the mask of Personality which you may happen to be wearing at this moment, or by the masks which are worn by those around you. Realize that back of your mask is the great Individual—the Indivisible—the Universal Life, in which you are a centre of consciousness and activity. This does not wipe out your identity—instead it gives you a greater and grander identity. Instead of your sinking into a Nirvana of extinction of consciousness, your consciousness so enlarges as you unfold, that you will in the end feel your identity to be the identity of the Universe. Instead of your gaining Nothingness, you gain Allness. All spiritual growth and unfoldment gives you a constantly increasing sense of relationship with, and agreement with, the All. You grow into Allness as you unfold. Be not deceived by this chatter about Nothingness, and loss of Individuality, in the Oriental thought, although some of the presentations of its teachings may so seem to mean at first reading. Remember always that Personality is the mask, and Individuality the Real One.

You have often heard persons, claiming to be acquainted with the teachings of Theosophy and other expositions of the Oriental Wisdom Religion (including our own presentation), asserting that the Oriental mind was ever bent upon attaining a final stage of Nothingness or Extinction in Nirvana. In addition to what we have said, and to what we shall say on this subject, let us quote from the inspired writer of the *"Secret Doctrine"* (a standard Theosophical work) when she says, in that work on page 286, Vol. I: "Is this annihilation, as some think? . . . To see in Nirvana annihilation, amounts to saying of a man plunged in a sound, dreamless sleep—one that leaves no impression on the physical memory and brain, because the sleeper's Higher Self is in its original state of absolute consciousness during these hours—that he too is annihilated. The latter simile answers only to one side of the question—the most material; since reabsorption is by no means such a dreamless sleep, but, on the contrary, absolute existence, an unconditional unity, or a state, to describe which human language is absolutely and hopelessly inadequate. . . . Nor is the individuality —nor even the essence of the personality, if any be left behind—lost because re-absorbed." As J. Wm. Lloyd says, in connection with the above quotation, "This seems conclusive proof that Theosophy does not regard Nirvana as annihilation, but as an infinite enlargement of consciousness." And we would add that this is true not only as regards the Nirvana of the Theosophist, but also of the consciousness of the Unity of Life—the Universal Life. This too is not annihilation of individual consciousness, but an "infinite enlargement of consciousness" as this Western writer Lloyd has so well expressed it.

The very consciousness of Life that every man feels within him, comes not from something belonging exclusively to himself as a separate or personal thing. On the contrary, it belongs to his Individuality, not to his Personality, and is a phase of his consciousness or "awareness" of his relation to the One Universal Life which underlies his existence, and in which he is a center of consciousness. Do you grasp this idea? If not, meditate and concentrate upon it, for it is important. You must learn to *feel* the Life within you, and to know that it is the Life of the great Ocean of Universal Life upon the bosom of which you are borne as a centre of consciousness and energy. In this thought there is Power, Strength, Calm, Peace, and Wisdom. Acquire it, if you are wise. It is indeed a Gift from the Gods.

In this lesson we are not attempting to build up

your idea of the Unity of Life by a series of arguments taken from a world of phenomena in which separateness and non-Unity is apparent. No such arguments would suffice, for it would be like trying to prove the existence and laws of color to a man born blind, by arguments taken from his world of darkness. On the contrary we are appealing to that region of the mind in which is stored the capacity for intuitively apprehending truth. We are endeavoring to speak in tones which will awaken a similar vibration in that part of your mentality, and if these vibrations be started into being, then will you be able to *feel* and *know* the truth, and then will your Intellect eagerly seize upon the new idea that it finds within itself, and will proceed to apply the same to the various problems that have been bothering you in the past.

This consciousness of Unity must come from the higher regions of the mind, for the Intellect alone knows it not,—it is out of its field. Just as one may not know that the earth is round by means of his senses which report quite the contrary, but may and does know this truth by abstract reasoning and higher intellectual effort; so may one know the truth that All Life is indeed One, at the last, and underlying, by the higher faculties of the mind, although his senses and ordinary intellectual processes fail to so inform him. The senses cannot inform man that the earth is round, *because they cannot see it as a whole, but only in part* —while the higher reasoning faculties are able to visualize the earth as a whole, and know it must be round. And the Intellect, in its ordinary field can see only separateness, and cannot report Oneness, but the Higher Mind sees Life as a Whole, and knows it to be One. And it is the Higher Mind that we are trying to bring into the field of consciousness in the appeal to you in this lesson. We trust that we may be successful—in fact we *know* that we shall be so, in many cases, for we know that the field is ready for the sowing of the seed—and that the call has been heard, and the message passed on to us to answer the call—else these words would not have been written.

The consciousness of the Unity of Life is something that must be experienced before the truth may be realized. It is not necessary for one to wait until he acquire full Cosmic Consciousness before he may realize, at least partially, the Oneness of All Life, for he may unfold gradually into the Cosmic Knowing, experiencing at each stage a fuller conception of the underlying Unity of Life, in which he is a centre of consciousness and manifestation. But there must be at least a partial unfoldment before one is able to *feel* the sense of Unity. To those who have not unfolded sufficiently to gain at least a glimmering of the truth, everything appears separate from every other thing, and there is no Unity of All. It is as if every leaf on a mighty tree were to consider itself a being separate and distinct from everything else in the world, failing to perceive its connection with the branch or limb, and tree, and its unity in being with every other leaf on the tree. After a bit the unfolding consciousness of the leaf enables it to perceive the stem that connects it with the twig. Then it begins to realize certain relationships, and feels its vital connection with the twig and the few other leaves attached to the same twig. Later on, it unfolds sufficiently to perceive that certain other leaf-bearing twigs are connected with the same branch, and it learns to feel its relationship with all twigs and leaves springing from that branch. Then again, a little later on, it begins to realize that other branches spring from the same limb as its branch, and the sense of relationship and dawning Unity begins to widen still further. And so it goes on, until at last, the tiny leaflet realizes that the life of the tree is the life of all of its parts—limbs, branches, twigs, leaves, blossoms, fruit, seed, etc., and that it, itself, is but a centre of expression in the One Life of the tree. Does the leaf feel less important and real from this discovery? We should say assuredly not, for it must feel that behind its tiny form and limited strength is the strength and vitality of the entire organism of the tree. It must know that the tree is ever at work extracting nourishment from the earth, air, and water, and transmitting that nourishment to its every part, including our little friend the leaflet. It knows that the sap will rise in the Spring to renew the manifestations of life, and it knows that although its leafy form may wither and die, still the essence of its life—its real Life—does not die but remains ever active and strong awaiting its chance for future expression and re-embodiment. Of course this figure of the leaf and the tree fails us if we attempt to carry it very far, but it will give us at least a partial idea of the relationship between the life of the person, and the One Life.

Some of the Oriental teachers have illustrated this idea to their students by various familiar examples and figures of speech. Some bid the student hold up his hand, and then point out to him that each finger is apparently separate and distinct if one does not look down to where it joins the hand. Each finger, if it had consciousness, might well argue that it was a separate individual, having no relationship with any other finger. It might prove this to its own satisfaction, and to that of its listeners, by showing that it could move itself without stirring the other fingers. And so long as its consciousness was confined to its upper two joints it would remain under the illusion of separateness. But when its consciousness at last permeated the depths of its being, it would find that it emerged from the same hand from which also sprung the other fingers, and that its real life and power was vested in the hand rather than in itself, and that although apparently separate and independent, it was really but a part of the hand. And when its consciousness, through the consciousness of the hand, broadened and widened, it would perceive its relationship with, and interdependence with, the whole body, and would also recognize the power of the brain, and its mighty Will.

Another favorite illustration of the Eastern teachers is the stream of water flowing over a rocky bed. They point to the stream before it comes to a rocky place, and show the *chela* (student) that it is One. Then they will move a little way down the stream and show him how the rocks and stones divide the stream into countless little streams, each of which might imagine itself a separate and distinct stream, until later on it again joins the main united stream, and finds that it was but a form of expression of the One.

Another illustration that is frequently used by the teachers, is that which bids the student consider himself as a minute cell, or "little-life" as the Hindus call it, in a body. It may bė a cell in the blood performing the office of a carrier or messenger, or it may be a working cell in one of the organs of the body; or it may be a thinking cell in the brain. At any rate, the cell manifests capacity for thought, action and memory—and a number of secondary attributes quite wonderful in the way. (See *"Hatha Yoga,"* Chapter XVIII.) Each cell might well consider itself as a separate individual—in a certain sense it *does*. It has a certain degree of something akin to consciousness, enabling it to perform its work correctly and properly, and is called upon at times to manifest something like judgment. It may well be excused for thinking of itself as a "person" having a separate life. The analogy between its illusions and that of the man when seen by a Master, is very close. But we know that the life of the cell is merely a centre of expression of the life of the body—that its consciousness is merely a part of the consciousness of the mind animating the body. The cell will die and apparently perish, but the *essence* of it will remain in the life of the person whose body it occupied, and nothing really dies or perishes. Would the cell feel any less real if it knew that behind its Personality as a cell, there was the Individuality of the Man—that its Real Self was the Man, not the cell? Of course, even this figure of speech can be carried only so far, and then must stop, for the personality of the man, when it is dissolved, leaves behind it an essence which is called Character, which becomes the property of the Ego and which accompanies it into after life according to the Law of Karma, of which we shall speak in future lessons. But back even of these attributes of Personality, is the Ego which exists in spite of Personality, and lives on and on throughout many Personalities, and yet learning the lessons of each, until at last it rises above Personality and enters into higher sphere of Knowing and Being.

Still another favorite illustration of the Hindu teachers is that of the sun beating down upon the ocean and causing a portion of the water to rise in the form of vapor. This vapor forms clouds which spread all over the earth, and which eventually condense in the form of rain drops, dew, etc. This rain and dew form streams, rivers, etc., and sooner or later every drop finds its way back to Mother Ocean which is its Real Self. Separate though the dewdrop be, yet it is a part of the Ocean, no matter how far distant it may be, and the attraction of the Ocean will surely, and without fail, draw it back to its bosom. And the dewdrop, if it could know the truth, would be so much happier and stronger, and braver if it could know that it was superior to accident, time and space, and that it could not escape its own good, and that nothing could prevent its final triumph and victory when at last "the dewdrop glides into the shining sea." How cheerfully it could have met its many changes of form, and the incidents of its journey, if it could have gotten rid of the illusion of separateness, and knew that instead of being a tiny insignificant dewdrop it was a part of the Mighty Ocean—in fact that its Real Self was that Ocean itself—and that the Ocean was continually drawing it toward it, and that the many changes, up and down, were in response to that mighty power of attraction which was slowly but irresistibly drawing it back Home to Rest, Peace, and Power.

As valuable as are all these illustrations, examples, and figures of speech, still all must of necessity fall short of the truth in the case of the Soul of Man—that wondrous something which has been built up by the Absolute after aeons and aeons of time, and which is destined to play an important part in the great Cosmic Drama which it has pleased the Absolute to think into existence. Drawing its Life from the Universal Life, it has the roots of its being still further back in the Absolute itself, as we shall see in the next lesson. Great and wonderful is it all, and our minds are but illy fitted to receive the truth, and must be gradually accustomed to the glare of the Sun. But it will come to all—none can escape his glorious destiny.

The Oriental writings are full of allusions to the underlying Oneness, in fact the entire Oriental philosophies rest upon it. You may find it everywhere if you will but look for it. The experience of Cosmic Consciousness, which is naught but a sudden or gradual "awareness" of the underlying Unity of Life, is evidenced everywhere in the *Upanishads,* that wonderful series of teachings in the Hindu classics. Every writer in the collection gives his evidence regarding this awareness of Unity and Oneness, and the experiences and mental characteristics arising from the same. The following quotations will give an idea of the prevalence of this thought:

"He that beholds all beings in the Self, and the Self in all things, he never turns away from it."

"When to a man who understands, the Self has become all things, what sorrow, what trouble, can there be to him who once beheld that unity."

The Hindu father explains to his son that the One Life is in all forms and shapes, points out object after object, saying to the boy: "*Tat tvam asi,* Thou art that; That thou art."

And the Mystics have added their testimony to that of others who have experienced this consciousness. Plotinus said: "Knowledge has three degrees: opinion, science, and illumination. The last is absolute knowledge founded upon the identity of the knowing mind with the known object."

And Eckhardt, the German mystic, has told his pupils that: "God is the soul of all things. He is the light that shines in us when the veil is rent."

And Tennyson, in his wonderful verse describing the temporary lifting of the veil for him, has described a phase of Cosmic Consciousness in the following words:

"For knowledge is the swallow on the lake
That sees and stirs the surface-shadow there,
But never yet hath dippt into the abysm,
The Abysm of all Abysms, beneath, within
The blue of sky and sea, the green of earth,
And in the million-millionth of a grain
Which cleft and cleft again for evermore
And ever vanishing, never vanishes. . . .
And more, my son, for more than once when I
Sat all alone, revolving in myself
That word which is the symbol of myself,
The mortal symbol of the Self was loosed,
And past into the Nameless, as a cloud
Melts into Heaven. I touched my limbs, the limbs
Were strange, not mine—and yet no shadow of doubt,
But utter clearness, and through loss of Self
The gain of such large life as matched with ours
Were Sun to spark, unshadowable in words,
Themselves but shadows of a shadow-world."

And not only among the mystics and poets is this universal truth experienced and expressed, but among the great philosophers of all ages may we find this teaching of the Unity of Life originally voiced in the *Upanishads*. The Grecian thinkers have expressed the thought; the Chinese philosophers have added their testimony; the modern philosophers, Spinoza, Berkeley, Kant, Hegel, Schopenhauer, Hartman, Ferrier, Royce, although differing widely in their theories, all have expressed as a fundamental truth the Unity of Life—a One Life underlying. The basic teachings of the Vedas are receiving confirmation at the hands of Modern Science, which while calling itself Rationalistic and inclining to a Materialistic conception of the Universe, still finds itself compelled to say, "At the last, All is One."

And in nearly every human soul there is a secret chamber in which the text of this knowledge lies hidden, and in the rare moments in which the chamber door is opened in response to poetry, music, art, deep religious feeling, or those unaccountable waves of uplift that come to all, the truth is recognized for the moment and the soul feels at peace and is content in the feeling that it is at harmony with the All. The sense of Beauty, however expressed, when keenly experienced, has a tendency to lift us out of our consciousness of separateness into another plane of mind in which the keynote is Unity. The higher the human feeling, the nearer is the conscious realization of the underlying Unity.

This realization of the Unity of Life—the Oneness of Life—the Great Life—even when but faintly experienced, renders Life quite a different thing to the person. He feels no longer that he is a mere "part" of something that may be destroyed—or that he is a tiny personal something, separate from and opposed to all the rest of the Universe—but that he is, instead, a Unit of Expression—a Centre of Consciousness—in the Great One Life. He realizes that he has the Power, and Strength, and Life, and Wisdom of the Whole back of him, upon which he may learn to draw as he unfolds. He realizes that he is at Home, and that he cannot be thrust out, for there is no outside of the All. He feels within himself the certainty of infinite Life and being, for his Life is the all Life, and that cannot die. The petty cares, and worries, and griefs, and pains of everyday personal life are seen for what they are, and they cease to threaten and dominate him as of old. He sees the things of personality as merely the costume and trappings of the part in the play of life that he is acting out, and he knows that when he discards them he will still be "I."

When one really feels the consciousness of the One Life underlying, he acquires a confident trust and faith, and a new sense of freedom and strength comes to him, for is he not indeed delivered from the bondage of fear that has haunted him in his world of separateness. He feels within him the spiritual pulse of the Universal Life, and at once he thrills with a sense of new-found power and being. He becomes reconciled with Life in all its phases, for he knows these things as but temporary phases in the working out of some great Universal plan, instead of things permanent and fixed and beyond remedy. He begins to feel the assurance of Ultimate Justice and God, and the old ideas of Injustice and Evil begin to fade from him. He who enters into the consciousness of the Universal Life, indeed enters into a present realization of the Life Everlasting. All fear of being "lost" or "eternally damned" fades away, and one instinctively realizes that he is "saved" because he is of the One Life and cannot be lost. All the fear of being lost arises from the sense of illusion of separateness or apartness from the One Life. Once the consciousness of Unity is gained, fear drops from the soul like a wornout garment.

When the idea and consciousness of the Unity takes possession of one, he feels a new sense of cheerfulness and optimism entirely different from any other feeling that he has ever experienced. He loses that distrust and hardness which seems to cling to so many in this age who have arrived at the Intellectual stage of development, and have been unable to progress further. A new sense of peace and harmony comes to one, and illuminates his entire character and life. The bitterness engendered by the illusion of separateness is neutralized by the sweetness of the sense of Unity. When one enters into this consciousness he finds that he has the key to many a riddle of life that has heretofore perplexed him. Many dark corners are illuminated

—many hard sayings are made clear. Paradoxes become understandable truths, and the pairs of opposites that dwell in all advanced intellectual conceptions, seem to bend around their ends and form themselves into a circle.

To the one who understands the Unity, all Nature seems akin and friendly. There is no sense of antagonism or opposition—everything is seen to fit into its place, and work out its appointed task in the Universal plan. All Nature is seen to be friendly, when properly understood, and Man regains that sense of harmonious environment and at-home-ness that he lost when he entered the stage of self-consciousness. The lower animal and the children feel this Unity, in their poor imperfect way, but Man lost this Paradise when he discovered Good and Evil. But Paradise Lost becomes Paradise Regained when Man enters into this new stage of consciousness. But unlike the animal or child, which instinctively feels the Unity, the awakened soul of man possesses the Unity consciousness, coupled with intelligent comprehension, and unfolding spiritual power. He has found that which he lost, together with the accumulated interest of the ages. This new kingdom of Consciousness is before the race. All must enter into it in time—all will enter into it—many are entering into it now, by gradual stages. This dawning sense of Unity is that which is causing the spiritual unrest which is now agitating the world, and which in time will bring the race to a realization of the Fatherhood of God and the Brotherhood of Man, and his kinship to Every Living Thing. We are entering into this new cycle of human unfoldment, and the greatest changes are before the race. Ye who read these words are in the foremost ranks of the new dispensation, else you would not be interested in this subject. You are the leaven which is designed to lighten the heavy mass of the world-mind. Play well your parts. You are not alone. Mighty forces and great Intelligences are behind you in the work. Be worthy of them. Peace be with you.

Carry with you the Central Thought of this lesson:

CENTRAL THOUGHT. *There is but One Life —a Universal Life—in the world. This One Life is an emanation from the Absolute. It infills all forms, shapes and manifestations of Life, and is the Real Life that each imagines to be his personal property. There is but One—and you are centres of consciousness and expression in that One. There is a Unity and Harmony which becomes apparent to those who enter into the consciousness of the One Life. There is Peace and Calm in the thought. There is Strength and Power in the knowledge. Enter ye into your Kingdom of Power—possess yourselves of your Birthright of Knowledge. In the very center of your being you will find a holy of holies in which dwells the Consciousness of the One Life, underlying. Enter into the Silence of the Shrine within.*

THE FIFTH LESSON

THE ONE AND THE MANY.

As we have stated in previous Lessons, all philosophies which thinkers have considered worthy of respect, find their final expression of Truth in the fundamental thought that there is but *One Reality,* underlying all the manifold manifestations of shape and form. It is true that the philosophers have differed widely in their conception of that One, but, nevertheless, they have all agreed upon the logical necessity of the fundamental conception that there is, at least, but One Reality, underlying All.

Even the Materialists have conceded this conclusion, and they speak and think of a something called "Matter," as the One—holding that, inherent in Matter, is the potentiality of all Life. The school of Energists, holding that Matter in itself is non-existent, and that it is merely a mode of manifestation of a something called "Energy," asserts that this something called Energy is One, fundamental, real, and self-sufficient.

The various forms of Western religious thought, which hold to the various conceptions of a Personal Deity, also hold to a Oneness, inasmuch as they teach that in the beginning there was God, only, and that all the Universe has been *created* by Him. They do not go into details regarding this creation, and, unlike the Oriental teachers, they fail to distinguish between the conception of the *creation of shape and form,* on the one hand; and the *creation of the substance of these shapes and forms,* on the other hand. But, even accepting the premises of these people who hold to the Personal Deity conception, it will be seen that the Reason requires the acceptance of one or two ideas, *viz.,* (1) That the Deity created the substance of these shapes and forms from *Nothing;* or else (2) that he created them out of *his own substance*—out of Himself, in fact. Let us consider, briefly, these two conceptions.

In the first conception, *i. e.,* Creation from Nothing, we are brought face to face with an impregnable obstacle, inasmuch as the human reason positively refuses to think of Anything coming from Nothing. While it is perfectly true that the finite human mind cannot undertake to limit the powers of the Infinite; or to insist that the possibilities of the Divine Power must be measured and limited by the finite power of Man—still it must hearken to the report of its own highest faculties, and say "I cannot Think it," or else blindly accept the teachings of other finite minds which are equally unable to "Think it," and which have no superior sources of information. The Infinite Power has endowed us with reasoning faculties, and evidently expects us to use them to their full capacity—else the gift were a mockery. And in the absence of information from higher sources than the Reason, we must use the Reason in thinking of this matter, or else refuse to think of it at all.

In view of the above thought, let us then consider the report of the Reason, regarding this matter. And then, after having done so, let us apply the test of this report of the Reason, to the highest teaching of the Yogi Philosophy, and see how the latter stands the test. And, after having done this, we will apply the test of the Higher Consciousness to the same teachings. Remember this always, that while there is knowledge that transcends Reason—that is knowledge that comes from the Higher Regions of the Mind—still even such information of the Spiritual Mind *does not run contrary to Reason,* although it goes beyond it. There is harmony between the Spiritual Mind and the Highest Reason.

Returning to the consideration of the matter of Creation of Substance from Nothing, we again assert that *the Reason is unable to think of the creation of Something from Nothing.* It finds the statement unthinkable, and contrary to all the laws of thought. It is true that the Reason is compelled to accept as a final truth, many things that it cannot *understand* by reason of its finitude—but this is not one of them. There is no logical necessity for the Reason to accept any such conception as this—there is no warrant in the Reason for any such theory, idea or conclusion. Let us stop here, for a moment, and examine into this difference—it may help us to think clearer, hereafter.

We find it impossible to *understand* the fact of the Infinite Being having always existed—and Being without Cause. We find it impossible to conceive of the nature of an Eternal, Causeless, and Infinite Being—to conceive the *nature of,* such a Being, remember.

But, while this is so, still our Reason, by its own laws, compels us to think that there *must be* such a Being, so long as we think at all. For, if we think at all, we *must* think of there being a Fundamental Reality—and we *must* think of that Reality as being without Cause (because there can be no Cause for the First Cause); and we *must* think of that Reality as being Eternal (because It could not have sprung into Being from Nothing, and therefore must have always been); and we *must* think of that Reality as Infinite (because there is nothing outside of Itself to limit It). Think over this statement for a moment—until you grasp it fully.

But there is no such necessity, or compulsion, in the case of the question of Creation from Nothingness. On the contrary, the necessity and compulsion is all the other way. Not only is the Reason unable to *think of* Creation from Nothing—not only does all its laws forbid it to hold such a conception—but, more than this, it finds within itself a conception, full-grown and potent, which contradicts this idea. It finds within itself the strong certainty that *Whatever Really Is has Always Been*, and that all transient and finite shapes, forms, and manifestations, *must* proceed from that which is Real, Infinite, Causeless, and Infinite—and moreover *must be composed of the substance of that Reality*, for there is nothing else Real from which they could have been composed; and their composition from Nothing is unthinkable, for Nothing is Nothing, and always will be Nothing. "Nothing" is merely a name of denial of existence—an absolute denial of substantiality of any degree, kind or form—an absolute denial of Reality. And from such could come only Nothing—from Nothing, Nothing comes.

Therefore, finding within itself the positive report that All, and Anything There Is, must be composed of the Substance of the Reality, the Reason is compelled to think that the Universe is composed of the Substance of the One Reality—whether we call that One Reality, by the name of The Absolute; or whether we call it God. *We must believe that from this Absolute-God all things in the Universe have flown out, or been emanated, rather than created—begotten, rather than "made."*

This does not mean the Pantheistic idea that the Universe *is* God—but rather that God, while existing separate and apart from His Universe, in his Essence, and Being, is nevertheless *in* His Universe, and His Universe *in* Him. And this, no matter what conception of God or Deity is had—or whether one thinks of The Absolute as Principle. The Truth is the same—Truth no matter by what names it is called, or by what misconception it is surrounded. The Truth is that *One is in All, and All is in One*—such is the report of the highest Reason of Man—such is the report of the Illumined—such is the Highest Teachings that have come down to the race from the great souls that have trodden The Path of Attainment.

And now let us submit the Yogi Philosophy to these conceptions, and reports of the Reason. And let us discover just what more the Yogi Philosophy has to say concerning the *nature of* the Substance of the Divine, which infills all Life—and how it solves the Riddle of the Sphinx, concerning the One in All; and All in One. We hope to show you that the Riddle is capable of solution, and that the old Yogi teachers have long ago grasped that for which the human mind has ever sought. This phase of the Teachings is the highest, and it is usually hinted at, rather than expressed, in the writings on the subject—owing to danger of confusion and misconception. But in these Lessons we shall speak the Truth plainly, and without fear—for such is the Message which has been given us to deliver to our students—and we will perform the Right action, leaving the Result, or Fruits of the Action, where it belongs, according to the higher teachings found in the "*Bhavagad Gita*," and in the Higher Teachings of the Yogi Philosophy.

The fundamental Truth embedded in the Wisdom-Philosophies of the East—the Higher Yogi Teachings—is the impregnable doctrine of the One Self in the many selves—the many selves in the One Self. This fundamental Truth underlies all the Oriental Philosophies which are esoteric in their nature.

Notwithstanding the crude and often repulsive conceptions and practices of the masses of the people who represent the exoteric, or popular, phase of the teachings (and these two phases are to be found in *all* regions) still there is always this Inner Doctrine of the One Self, to be found to those who look for it.

Not only is this true among the Hindus; but even among the Mahommedans, of all countries, there is an Inner Circle of Mystics, known as the *Sufis,* holding to this Truth. And the inner teachings of the philosophies of all ages and races, have held likewise. And the highest thought of the philosophers of the Western races, has found refuge in this idea of the Oversoul, or Universal Self. But, it is only among the Yogis that we find an attempt made to explain the real nature of the manifestation of the One in Many—the holding of the Many forms in the One Self.

Before proceeding to the consideration of *how* the One becomes as Many, as expounded by the Higher Yogi Teachings, it becomes necessary to speak of a matter upon which there has been much confusion and misunderstanding, not only on the part of the students of various Oriental Philosophies, but also upon the part of some of the teachers themselves. We allude to the connection between THE ONE—THE ABSOLUTE—in Its ESSENCE—and that which has been called the One Life; the Universal Life, etc.

Many writers have spoken of the Universal Life, and The One, as being identical—but such is a grievous error, finding no warrant in the Highest Yogi Teachings. It is true that all living forms dwell in, and are infilled with the Universal Life—that All Life is One. We have taught this truth, and it is indeed Truth, without qualification. But there is still a Higher Truth—the Highest Truth, in fact—and that is, that even this Universal Life is not the One, but, instead, is in itself a manifestation of, and emanation from, THE ONE. There is a great difference here—see that you perceive and understand it, before proceeding further.

THE ONE—THE ABSOLUTE—according to the Highest Teachings, is Pure Spirit, and not Life, Mind, or Being as we understand them in our finite and mortal expressions. But, still all Life, Mind, and Being, as we understand them, spring from, flow from, and emanate from, the One—and more than this, may be spoken of as *reflections* of the Life, Mind, and Being of The One, if we may be permitted to apply the names of finite manifestations to the Infinite Reality.

So, the Highest Teaching is that the Universal Life infilling all living things, is not, in itself, the Being and Life of THE ONE—but is rather a great fundamental emanation of The One, the manner and nature of which will be spoken of as we proceed. Remember this, please.

Leading up to the Supreme Idea of the One in All—All in One—let us examine into the report of the Reason upon the *nature of* the Substance—the Divine Substance—from which all living forms are shaped; and from which all that we know as Finite Mind is likewise composed. *How can these imperfect and finite forms be composed of a Divine and Perfect Substance?* This is the question that must occur to the minds of those who are capable of deep thought on the subject—and it is a question that must be answered. And it can be answered—and *is* answered in the Higher Yogi Philosophy. Let us examine the reports of the Reason, a little further—then shall we be ready for the Teachings.

Of what can the Substance of the Infinite be composed? Can it be Matter? Yes, if you are satisfied with the reasoning of the Materialists, and cannot see further into the Truth! These teach that Matter is God, and that God is Matter. But if you be among those who reject the Materialistic teachings, you will not be satisfied with this answer. Even if you incline toward a Non-mental Infinite, still if you are familiar with the results of modern scientific investigation, and know that Science has seen Matter resolve itself into something like Electric Energy, you will know that the Truth must lie behind and beyond Matter.

Then is it Pure Energy? you may ask. Pure Energy? what's that? Can you think of Energy apart from material manifestation? Have you ever known of such a thing? Do you not know that even the Electron Theory, which is attracting the attention of advanced Modern Science, and which holds that all things are composed of minute particles of Electric Energy, called Electrons, from which the Atoms are built—do you not know that even this theory recognizes the necessity of a "something like Matter, only infinitely finer," which they call the Ether, to enfold the Electric Energy as a unit—to give it a *body,* as it were? And can you escape from the fact that the most advanced scientific minds find confronting them

—the fact that in all Energy, and governing its actions, there is manifested "something like Mind"?

And does not all this teach thinkers that just as Energy creates from itself, that which is called Matter, and then uses it as a vehicle of expression and action—so does this "Something like Mind" create from itself that which we call Energy, and proceeds to use it, with its accompanying phase of Matter, for its expression? Does not all advanced research show us that in all Matter and Energy there are evidences of the operation of this "Something like Mind"? And if this be so, are we not justified as regarding Matter and Energy as mere Effects—and to look to this "Something like Mind" as the more fundamental Substance? We think so—and Science is beginning to think so, too. And soon will Science be regarding with the most profound respect, the Metaphysical axiom that "All is Mind."

You will see by reference to our *"Advanced Course in Yogi Philosophy, etc.,"* the general Yogi teachings regarding the Emanation of the One, known respectively as Mind, Energy, and Matter. You will see that the Yogis teach that Mind, Energy, and Matter comprise a threefold emanation of the Absolute. You will also see that it is taught that Mind was the Parent-Emanation—the Universal Mind; and that the Universal Energy was the Second-Emanation (proceeding from Mind); and that the Universal Matter was the Third Emanation (proceeding from Energy). In the same book you will find that the Teaching is that above Matter, Energy, and Mind, is the Essence of the Absolute, which is called Spirit—the nature of which is non-understandable to the mind of Man, the highest conception of which is the highest manifestation of itself—Mind. But as we cannot comprehend spirit otherwise, we are justified in thinking of it as Something like Infinite Mind—Something as much higher than Finite Mind as that is higher than mere energy.

Now, then—we have seen the folly of thinking of the Divine Substance as Matter or Energy. And we have come to know it as Spirit, something like Mind, only infinitely higher, but which still may be thought of in terms of Infinite Mind, for we can have no higher terms in our thinking operations. So we may then assume that this Divine Nature or substance is SPIRIT, which we will think of as Infinite Mind, for want of a better form of conception.

We have seen the folly of thinking of the Divine Essential Substance as the Body of God. We have likewise seen the folly of thinking of it as the Vital Energy of God. And we have found that we could not escape thinking of it as the Spirit, or infinite Mind of God. Beyond this we cannot think intelligently.

But do you not see that all this exercise of the Reason has brought us to the point where we must think that this Divine Substance, which the Absolute-God uses in the manifestation of Universal Life; the Universe; and all the forms, and shapes, and manifestations of life and things in the Universe—this Divine Substance which must be *in* All Things—and *in which* All Things must rest, even as the bubble rests on the Ocean—that this can be nothing less than Spirit, and that this Spirit can be thought of only as Infinite Mind?

And, if this be so, then indeed must *All be Mind, and Mind be All*—meaning, of course, the Infinite Mind, not the finite manifestation that we *call* Mind.

Then, if this reasoning has been correct, then must we think that All Life—all the Universe—Everything except the Absolute itself—*must be held in the Infinite Mind of the Absolute!*

And, so, by the exercise of our Reason—by listening to, and examining its reports, we have been brought face to face—eye to eye—heart to heart—with the Teaching of the Illumined Ones, which has come down to us as the Highest Teaching of the Yogi Philosophy! For this, indeed, is the highest conception of Truth in the Yogi Teachings—this, that ALL MANIFESTATIONS AND EMANATIONS OF THE ABSOLUTE ARE MENTAL CREATIONS OF THE ABSOLUTE — THOUGHT-FORMS HELD IN THE INFINITE MIND—THE INFINITE SPIRIT IN THEM—AND THEY IN THE INFINITE SPIRIT. *And that the only Real Thing about Man is THE SPIRIT involved in the Thought-Form, the rest is mere Personality, which changes and ceases to be. The Spirit in the Soul of Man, is the SOUL OF THE SOUL, which is never born; never changeth; never dieth—this is The Real Self of*

Man, in which, indeed, he is "One with the Father."

This is the point where the Reasoning Mind of Man has come to a sense of Agreement with the Highest Yogi Teachings. Let us now pass on to the Teachings themselves—let us listen to The Message of Truth.

In this consideration of the Highest Yogi Philosophy, and its teaching, we would again say to our students, that which we said to them in "*The Advanced Course*"—that we do not attempt to teach the "why" of the Manifestation of The Absolute, but rest content with delivering the Message of the Yogi Sages, which deals with the "how." As we stated in the lessons referred to, we incline to that school of the Higher Teachings, which holds that the "Why" of the Infinite Manifestation must, of necessity, rest with the Infinite alone, and that the finite mind cannot hope to answer the question. We hold that in all the Universal Mind, or in any of its Mind Manifestations, there is to be found no answer to this question! Wrapped in the Essence of the Absolute Spirit, alone, is this Final Answer!

The Sages, and Masters, from their high spiritual points of observation, possess many truths regarding the "how" side of the question that would appear almost like Infinite Wisdom itself, compared with our puny knowledge. But even these great souls report that they do not possess the answer to the Final Question—the "Why" of the Infinite Manifestation. And so we may be excused from attempting to answer it—and without shame or sense of shortcoming do we still say, to this question, "We do not know!"

In order that the Final Question may be fully understood let us consider it for a moment. We find the Question arising from the following condition:

The human Reason is compelled to admit that there is an Infinite, Eternal, Causeless REALITY underlying all forms of manifestation in the phenomenal world. It is likewise compelled to admit that this REALITY must comprise All that Really Is—and that there can be nothing Real outside of Itself. Arising from this is the Truth, that all forms of phenomenal manifestation, must emanate *from* the One Reality, for there is nothing else Real from which they could emanate. And the twin-Truth that these forms of manifestation, must also be *in* the Being of the One Reality, for there is nowhere outside of the All wherein they might find a place. So this One Reality is seen to be "That from which All Things flow"; and "That in which All Things live, and move and have their being."

Therefore All Things *emanate from,* and are *contained in* the One Reality. We shall consider "just how" later on, but the question which confronts us, and which has been called the "Final Question"—and that which we pronounce unanswerable—is this: "Why has the Infinite manifested and emanated Finite forms of being?" You will see the nature of the question when you stop to consider: (1) The Infinite cannot have Desire, for that is a Finite quality; (2)

It cannot lack anything, for that would take away from its Infinity; (3) and even if it did lack anything, from whence could it expect to acquire it; for there is nothing outside of itself—if It lacks anything, it must continue to always lack it, for there is no outside source from which It could obtain anything which it does not already possess. And Desire would be, of course, a *wanting* for something which it lacked—so It could not Desire unless it Lacked—and it would know that Desire would be hopeless, even if indeed it did Lack.

So you see that if we regard the Infinite Reality as Perfect, we must drop all ideas of It Desiring or Lacking—and of it Growing or Improving—or of it obtaining more Power, or Knowledge. These ideas are ridiculous, for an Absolute, Infinite Reality, must possess All-Knowledge; All-Power; All-Presence, else it is not Absolute and Infinite. And, if It does not possess these attributes of Being, then It can never hope to acquire them, for there is Nowhere from whence they could be acquired—there is no Source outside of the All-Source. A Finite Thing, may lack, and desire, and improve and develop, for there is the Universal Source from which it may draw. But the Infinite has no Universal Source, for it is Its own Source. Do you see the nature of the Final Question? If not we will again state it—it is this:

"Why should the Infinite Reality, which possesses all that may be possessed ,and which in itself is the only Source of Things—WHY should It Desire to manifest a Universe from and within Itself?"

A little consideration will show you that there is no intelligent answer to the "Why," either in your own minds, or in the writings and teachings of the greatest minds. The matter is important, to those who are confronted every day with some of the many attempts to answer this Final Question—it is well that our students inform them regarding the futility of such questioning. And with this end in view, we shall herein give a few of the wise "guesses" at the answer, and our reasons for considering them inadequate. We ask the student to consider carefully these remarks, for by so doing he will post himself, and will be saved much tedious and perplexing wandering along the dangerous places in the Swamp of Metaphysics, following the will-o'-the-wisp of Finite Mind masquerading as the Infinite Wisdom! Beware of the False Lights! They lead to the quagmire and quicksands of thought!

Let us now consider some of these "guesses" at the answer to the Final Question. Some thinkers have held that the Absolute was bound by a Divine Necessity to manifest itself as Many. The answer to this is that the Abs[illegible] could not be *bound* by anything, inner or outer, else it would not be Absolute and Infinite, but would be Relative and Finite. Another set of thinkers have held that the Absolute found within itself a Desire to Manifest as Many. From whence could come such an action-causing Desire? The Absolute could lack nothing, and there would be nothing for it to desire to gain, other than that which It already possessed. One does not desire things one already has, but only what he lacks.

Another school would tell us that the Infinite wished to *Express* itself in the phenomenal world. Why? Such a phenomenal world could only be reflection of Its power, witnessed only by Itself, and could contain nothing that was not already contained in the All. To what end would such a wish tend? What would be accomplished or gained? The Infinite All could not become anything more than It already was—so why the wish for expression? Some say that the whole phenomenal world is but *Maya,* or Illusion, and does not exist at all. Then who else than the Infinite caused the Illusion, and why the necessity? This answer only removes the question back one point, and does not really answer it. Some would say that the Universe is the "dream of the Infinite." Can we conceive the Infinite Being as exercisng the finite faculty of "dreaming"—is not this childish?

Others would have us believe that the Absolute is indulging in a "game" or "play," when he makes Universes, and those inhabiting them. Can anyone really believe this of The Absolute—playing like a child, with men and women, worlds and suns, as Its blocks and tin-soldiers? Why should the Infinite "play"?—does It need amusement and "fun" like a child? Poor Man, with his attempts to read the Riddle of the Infinite!

We know of teachers who gravely instruct their pupils in the idea that the Absolute and Infinite One manifests Universes and Universal Life, and all that flows from them, because It wishes to "gain experience" through objective existence. This idea, in many forms has been so frequently advanced that it is worth while to consider its absurdity. In the first place, what "experience" could be gained by the Absolute and Infinite One? What could It expect to gain and learn, that it did not already know and possess? One can gain experience only from others, and outside things—not from oneself entirely separated from the outside world of things. And there would be no "outside" for the Infinite. These people would have us believe that The Absolute emanated a Universe from Itself—which could contain nothing except that which was obtained from Itself—and then proceeded to gain experience from it. Having no "outside" from which it could obtain experiences and sentences and sensations, it proceeded to make (from Itself) an imitation one—that is what this answer amounts to. Can you accept it?

The whole trouble in all of these answers, or attempted answers, is that the answerer first conceives of the Absolute-Infinite Being, as a Relative-Finite Man, and then proceeds to explain what this Big Man would do. This is but an exaggerated form of anthropmorphism—the conception of God as a Man raised to great proportions. It is but an extension of the idea which gave birth to the savage conceptions of Deity as a cruel chief or mighty warrior, with human passions, hates, and revenge; love, passions, and desires.

Arising from the same cause, and akin to the theories advanced above are similar ones, which hold that the Absolute cannot dwell alone, but must forever bring forth souls from Itself—this was the idea of *Plotinus,* the Greek philosopher. Others have thought that the Infinite was possessed of such a consuming love, that It manifested objects upon which it could bestow Its affections. Others have thought that It was lonesome, and desired companionship. Some have spoken of the Absolute as "sacrificing" itself, in becoming Many, instead of remaining One. Others have taught that the Infinite somehow has become entangled in Its Manifestations, and had lost the knowledge of Its Oneness—hence their teachings of "I Am God." Others, holding to a similar idea, tell us that the Infinite is deliberately "masquerading" as the Many, in order to fool and mystify Itself—a show of Itself; by Itself, and for Itself! Is not this Speculative Metaphysics run wild? Can one in calm thought so regard the Infinite and Absolute Being—All-Wise—Causeless—All-Powerful — All-Present—All-Possessing—Lacking Nothing—Perfect One—as acting and performing thus, and from these motives? Is not this as childish as the childishness of the savage, and barbarians, in their Mumbo-Jumbo conceptions? Let us leave this phase of the subject.

The Higher Yogi Teachings hold to no such ideas or theories. It holds that the Answer to the Secret is vested in the Infinite alone, and that finite "guesses" regarding the "Why" are futile and pitiful. It holds that while one should use the Reason to the full, still there are phases of Being that can be considered only in Love, Faith, and Confidence in THAT from which All Things flow, and in which we live and move and have our being. It recognizes that the things of the Spirit, are known by the Mind. It explores the regions of the Universal Mind to its utmost limits, fearlessly—but it pauses before the Closed Door of The Spirit, reverently and lovingly.

But, remember this—that while the Higher Yogi Teachings contain no "guess," or speculative theory, regarding the "Why" of the Divine Manifestation, still they do not deny the existence of a "Why." In fact, they expressly hold that the Absolute Manifestation of the Many is in pursuance of some wondrous Divine Plan, and that the Unfoldment of the Plan proceeds along well-established and orderly lines, and according to Law. They trust in the Wisdom and Love of the Absolute Being, and manifest a perfect Confidence, Trust and Peaceful Patience in the Ultimate Justice, and Final Victory of the Divine Plan. No doubt disturbs this idea—it pays no attention to the apparent contradictions in the finite phenomenal world, but sees that all things are proceeding toward some far-away goal, and that "All is Well with the Universe."

But they do not think for a moment, or teach in the slightest degree, that all this Unfoldment, and Plan of the Universe, has for its object any advantage, benefit or gain to the Absolute—such a thought would be folly, for the Absolute is already Perfect, and Its Perfection cannot be added to, or taken away from. But they do positively teach that there is a great beneficial purpose in all the Plan, accruing in the end to the developed souls that have evolved through the workings of the plan. These souls do not possess the qualities of the Infinite—they are Finite, and thus are capable of receiving benefits; of growing, developing, unfolding, attaining. And, therefore, the Yogis teach that this building up of Great Souls seems to be the idea of the Infinite, so far as may be gained from an observation of the Workings of the Plan. The Absolute cannot *need these* Great Souls for Its own pleasure, and therefore their building-up must be for their own advantage, happiness and benefit.

The Yogis teach, on this subject, that there can be only ONE Real Perfect Being—Perfect without experience—Perfect from the Beginning—but only ONE! In other words, they teach that there can be no such thing as Absolute Perfection, outside of the Absolute Itself—and that not even the Absolute Being can create another Absolute Being, for in that case there would be no Absolute Being at all, but only *two Relative Beings.*

Think over this for a moment, and you will see its truth. The ABSOLUTE must always be "the One without a Second," as the Yogis express it—there cannot be *two* Perfect ones. And so, all Finite Beings, being Finite, must work their way up toward the plane of Perfection by The Path of Life, with all of its lessons, tasks, cares, pains, and strivings. This is the only way open to them—and even the Absolute cannot have it otherwise, and still be the Absolute. There is a fine point here—the Absolute is All-Powerful, but even that All-Power is not sufficient to enable It to destroy Its Absolute Being. And so, you who have wondered, perhaps you may now understand our words in the First Lesson of this series, in which we said that the message of the Absolute to some of the Illumined has been: "All is being done in the best and only possible way—I am doing the best I can—all is well—and in the end will so appear."

And, as we also said in that First Lesson: "The Absolute, instead of being an indifferent and unmoved spectator to its own creation, is a striving, longing, active, suffering, rejoicing, feeling Spirit, partaking of the feelings of Its manifestations, rather than callously witnessing them. It lives in us—with us—through us. Back of all the pain in the world, may be found a great feeling and suffering love." And in this thought there is comfort to the doubting soul—peace to the troubled mind.

In the Sixth Lesson, we shall proceed to deliver to you the further Message of Truth, concerning "how" the One Absolute manifests Its Mental Images as Universe; Universal Life; and Forms and Shapes; and Individualities, and Personalities. We had hoped to include the whole Message in this Fifth Lesson, but now find that we have merely laid the steps by which the student may reach the Essential Truth.

But, lest the student may be left in an uncertain state of mind, awaiting the conclusion of the consideration of the subject—and lest he may think that we intend teaching him that the Universe, and all in it, including himself are "Dreams," because we have said that All Things are Thought-Forms in the Mind of the Absolute—lest this misunderstanding may arise, we wish to add a few parting words to what we have said.

We wish to impress upon the mind of the student that though all Things are but Thought-Forms in the Mind of the Absolute Being, and that while it is true that the entire Universe of Universes is simply a Thought-Form held in the Mind of the Absolute—still this fact does not mean that all Things are "illusions" or "dreams." Remember this, now and forever, O Student—that that which is held in the Absolute Mind as a Thought-Form IS, and is all there IS, outside of the Absolute Itself. When the Absolute forms a Thought-Form, It forms it out of Its own mental substance—when the Absolute "holds anything in Its Mind," It holds it in Itself—for the Absolute is ALL-MIND.

The Absolute is not a material Being, from which Material Beings are created. It is a Spiritual Being—a Being whose Substance is akin to that which we call "Mind," only raised to Infinity and Absolute Perfection and Power. And this is the only way it can "create"—by creating a Thought-Form in Its Mental, or Spiritual Substance. The faintest "Thought" of the Absolute is more real and durable than anything that man can create—in fact, man can "create" nothing, for all the hard and real material he uses in his "creations," such as steel, diamonds, granite, are but some of the minor Forms, "thought" into being by the Absolute.

And also remember this, that the Absolute cannot "think" of anything, without putting Itself in that thing, as its Essence. Just as a man's Mental Images are not only *in* his mind, *but his mind is in them, also.*

Why, you doubting and timorous ones, does not even the finite "thinking" of Man manifest itself in physical and material changes of form and shape?—does not a man's every thought actually "create" physical forms and shapes, in his brain-cells and physical tissue? You who are reading these words—yea, *while* you are reading these words—are "creating" changes of form and shape in your brain-cells, and physical organism. Your mind is constantly at work, also, in building up your physical body, along the lines of the Instinctive Mind (see previous series of lessons)—you are mentally creating in a miniature universe, every moment of your life. And yet, the idea of the Absolute "creating" a Universe by pure Thought, in Its own Mind, and thereafter causing the work of the Universe to proceed according to Law, by simply "Willing" it so, causes you to wonder, and perhaps to doubt.

O, ye of little faith, you would deny to the Absolute even the power you possess yourself. You plan things in your mind every day, and then proceed to cause them to appear in material manifestation, and yet you doubt the ability of the Absolute to do likewise. Why even the poets, or writers of fiction, create characters in their minds—and these seem so real, that even you imagine them to be actual entities, and you weep over their pains, and smile at their joys—and yet all this is on the finite plane. Why, even the "imaginations" of your petty finite, undeveloped minds, have sufficient power to make your physical bodies sick, or well, or even to cause you to "die," from some imagined ailment. And yet you doubt the power of the Absolute, to "think" things into being! You tiny students in the great Kindergarten of Life—you must learn better lessons from your little blocks and games. And you *will*—this is the Law.

And you who are filled with the sense of your smallness, and "unreality"—know you that so long as you are "held in the Mind of God," then so long are you "remembered" by Him. And so long as you are remembered by Him, no real harm can befall you, and your Reality is second only to His own. Even though you pass out of your mortal frame—doth he remember you in His Mind, and keeping you there, he holds you safe and unharmed. The greatest satisfaction that can come to one, is to be able to fully realize that he, or she, is held firmly IN THE MIND OF THE INFINITE BEING. To such comes the knowledge that in THAT LIFE there can be NO DEATH.

Peace be with you in this Realization. May you make it your own!

THE SIXTH LESSON

WITHIN THE MIND OF THE ONE.

In our last lesson we gave you the Inner Teachings of the Yogi Philosophy, relating to the real nature of the Universe, and all that is therein contained. We trust that you have pondered well and carefully the statements contained in that lesson, for in them is to be found the essence of the highest Yogi teachings. While we have endeavored to present these high truths to you in the simplest possible form, yet unless your minds have been trained to grasp the thought, you may have trouble in fully assimilating the essence of the teachings. But, be not discouraged, for your mind will gradually unfold like the flower, and the Sun of Truth will reach into its inmost recesses. Do not be troubled if your comprehension seems dull, or your progress slow, for all things will come to you in time. You cannot escape the Truth, nor can the Truth escape you. And it will not come to you one moment sooner than you are ready to receive it, nor will it be delayed one moment in its coming, when you are ready for it. Such is the Law, and none can escape it, nor alter it, nor modify it. All is Well, and All is Under the Law—nothing ever "happens."

To many, the thought that the Universe and all that is therein contained, are simply "Thought Forms" in the Infinite Mind—Mental Creations of the Absolute, may seem startling, and a sense of unreality may pervade one. This is inevitable, but the reaction will come. To some who have grasped this mighty truth there has come a feeling that "All is Nothing," which idea is embodied in their teachings and writings. But this is merely the Negative Phase of the Truth—there is a Positive Phase which comes as one advances.

The Negative Phase shows us that all that we have considered as real and permanent—the foundations of the Universe itself—is but a mental image in the mind of the Absolute, and therefore lacks the fundamental reality that we had previously associated with it. And realizing this, we are at first apt to feel that, indeed "all is nothing," and to fall into a state of apathy, and lack of desire to play our part in the world. But, then, happily the reaction sets in, sooner or later, and we begin to see the Positive Phase of the Truth. This Positive Phase shows us that while all the forms, shapes, and phenomena of the Universe are but parts of a great show-world, still the *essence of* all must be Reality, itself, else there would not be even the "appearance" of a Universe. Before a thing can be a Mental Image, there must be a Mind to hold that Mental Image, and a BEING to possess that Mind. And, the very essence of that BEING must pervade and be immanent in every Image in that Mind. Just as *You* are really in your Mental Images, as well as they in You, so must the Absolute be *in* Its Mental Images, or Creations, or Thought Forms, as truly as they are in the Mind of the Absolute. Do you see this plainly? Think well over it—ponder it well—for in it lies the Truth.

And so, this Positive Phase of the Truth, is far

from depressing—it is the most stimulating conception that one can hold, if he but grasps it in its entirety and fulness. Even if it be true that all these shapes, and forms, and appearances, and phenomena, and personalities, be but illusion as compared to the inner Reality—what of it? Are you not then assured that the Spirit within Yourself is the Spirit of the Absolute—that the Reality within You is the Reality of the Absolute—that you ARE, because the Absolute IS, and cannot be otherwise? Does not the Peace, and Calm, and Security, and Bliss that comes to you with this Realization, far more than counterbalance the petty nothings that you have discarded? We think that there can be but one answer to this, when you have fully Realized the Truth.

What gives you the greatest Satisfaction and Content in Life? Let us see. Well, there is the Satisfaction of Immortality. The human mind instinctively craves this. Well, what that even the highest finite conceptions of Future Life have given you, can compare with the assurance of Actual Being, in and of the Absolute? What are your petty conceptions of "heavens," "paradises," "happy-hunting-grounds," "divine regions of the blessed," and the other ideas of the various religious sects, when compared with the conceptions of your Infinite and Eternal Existence in Spirit—your relation with The One—that conception of Infinite Wisdom, Being, and Bliss? When you grasp this truth, you will see that you are "in Eternity right Now," and are Immortal even this moment, as you have always been.

Now, what we have said above is not intended to deny the "heaven-worlds," or planes. On the contrary, you will find much in the teachings regarding these, which the Yogis enter into with much detail. But, we mean that back of all the "heavens" and "celestial planes," there is a still higher state of being —the "Absolute Being." Even the "heavens," and "heaven-worlds," and regions of the *Devas,* or Archangels, are but relative states—there is a state higher than even these exalted relative states, and that is the State of the Conscious Unity and Identity with the One. When one enters into that State, he becomes more than Man—more than gods—he is then "in the bosom of the Father."

And now, before proceeding to a consideration of the phenomenal manifestation of the Absolute—the evolving of the Universe in the Infinite Mind—we will again call your attention to the fact that underlies all the Universe of forms, shapes and appearances, and that is, as we stated in our last lesson:

All Manifestations and Emanations of the Absolute are Mental Creations of the Absolute—Thought-Forms held in the Infinite Mind—the Infinite Spirit in them —and they in the Infinite Spirit. And, the only Real Thing about Man is the Spirit involved in the Thought-Form—the rest is mere Personality, which changes and ceases to be. The Spirit in the Soul of Man, is the Soul of the Soul, which is never born; never changeth; never dieth—this is The Real Self of Man, in which, indeed, he is "One with the Father."

And, now let us consider the Yogi Teachings regarding the creation of the Universe, and the evolution of the living forms thereon. We shall endeavor to give you the story as plainly as may be, holding fast to the main thought, and avoiding the side-paths of details, etc., so far as is possible.

In the first place, we must imagine ourselves back to the beginning of a "Day of Brahm,"—the first dawn of that Day, which is breaking from the darkness of a "Night of Brahm." Before we proceed further, we must tell you something about these "Days and Nights of Brahm," of which you have seen much mention in the Oriental writings.

The Yogi Teachings contain much regarding the "Days and Nights of Brahm;" the "Inbreathing and Outbreathing of the Creative Principle;" the periods of "*Manvantara*," and the periods of "*Pralaya*." This thought runs through all the Oriental thought, although in different forms, and with various interpretations. The thought refers to the occult truth that there is in Cosmic Nature alternate periods of Activity and Inactivity—Days and Nights—Inbreathings and Outbreathings—Wakefulness and Sleep. This fundamental law manifests in all Nature, from Universes to Atoms. Let us see it now in its application to Universes.

At this point we would call the attention of the student that in many of the presentations of the Hindu Teachings the writers speak as if the Absolute, *Itself,* were subject to this law of Rhythm, and had Its

Periods of Rest and Work, like Its manifestations. This is incorrect. The highest teachings do not so hold, although at first glance it would so appear. The teaching really is that while the Creative Principle manifests this rhythm, still even this principle, great though it be, is a manifestation of the Absolute, and not the Absolute itself. The highest Hindu teachings are firm and unmistakable about this point.

And, another point, in which there is much mistaken teaching. In the periods of Creative Inactivity in a Universe it must not be supposed that there is no Activity anywhere. On the contrary, there is never a cessation of Activity on the part of the Absolute. While it is Creative Night in one Universe, or System of Universes, there is intense activity of Mid-Day in others. When we say "The Universe" we mean the Universe of Solar Systems—millions of such systems—that compose the particular universe of which we have any knowledge. The highest teachings tell us that this Universe is but one of a System of Universes, millions in number—and that this System is but one, in a higher System, and so on and on, to infinity. As one Hindu Sage hath said: "Well do we know that the Absolute is constantly creating Universes in Its Infinite Mind—and constantly destroying them—and, though millions upon millions of aeons intervene between creation and destruction, yet doth it seem less than the twinkle of an eye to The Absolute One."

And so the "Day and Night of Brahm" means only the statement of the alternating periods of Activity and Inactivity in some one particular Universe, amidst the Infinite Universality. You will find a mention of these periods of Activity and Inactivity in the "*Bhagavad Gita,*" the great Hindu epic. The following quotations, and page references, relate to the edition published by the Yogi Publication Society, which was compiled and adapted by the writer of these lessons. In that edition of the "*Bhagavad Gita,*" on page 77, you will find these words attributed to *Krishna,* the Absolute One in human incarnation:

"The worlds and universes—yea, even the world of Brahm, a single day of which is like unto a thousand *Yugas* (four billion years of the earth), and his night as much—these worlds must come and go. * * * The Days of Brahm are succeeded by the Nights of Brahm. In these Brahmic Days all things emerge from invisibility, and become visible. And, on the coming of the Brahmic Night, all visible things again melt into invisibility. The Universe having once existed, melteth away; and lo! is again re-created."

And, in the same edition, on page 80, we find these words, attributed to the same speaker:

"At the end of a *Kalpa*—a Day of Brahm—a period of Creative Activity—I withdraw into my nature, all things and beings. And, at the beginning of another *Kalpa,* I emanate all things and beings, and re-perform my creative act."

We may say here, in passing, that Modern Science now holds to the theory of periods of Rhythmic Change; of Rise and Fall; of Evolution and Dissolution. It holds that, beginning at some time in the past aeons of time, there was the beginning of an upward or evolutionary movement, which is now under way; and that, according to the law of Nature, there must come a time when the highest point will be reached, and then will come the beginning of the downward path, which in time must come to an end, being succeeded by a long period of inactivity, which will then be followed by the beginning of a new period of Creative Activity and Evolution—"a Day of Brahm."

This thought of this law of Rhythm, in its Universal form, has been entertained by the thinkers of all times and races. Herbert Spencer expressly held to it in his "First Principles," expressing it in many ways akin to this: "Evolution must come to a close in complete equilibrium or rest;" and again, "It is not inferable from the general progress towards equilibrium, that a state of universal quiescence or death will be reached; but that if a process of reasoning ends in that conclusion, a further process of reasoning points to renewals of activity and life;" and again, "Rhythm in the totality of changes—alternate eras of evolution and dissolution." The Ancient Western Philosophers also indulged in this idea. Heraclitus taught that the universe manifested itself in cycles, and the Stoics taught that "the world moves in an endless cycle, through the same stages." The followers of Pythagoras went even further, and claimed that "the succeeding worlds resemble each other, down to the minutest detail," this latter idea. however—the idea of the

"Eternal Recurrence"—while held by a number of thinkers, is not held by the Yogi teachers, who teach infinite progression—an Evolution of Evolution, as it were. The Yogi teachings, in this last mentioned particular, are resembled more by the line of Lotze's thinking, as expressed in this sentence from his *Microcosmos:* "The series of Cosmic Periods, * * * each link of which is bound together with every other; * * * the successive order of these sections shall compose the unity of an onward-advancing melody." And, so through the pages of Heraclitus, the Stoics, the Pythagoreans, Empedocles, Virgil, down to the present time, in Nietzche, and his followers, we find this thought of Universal Rhythm—that fundamental conception of the ancient Yogi Philosophy.

And, now, returning to the main path of our thought —let us stand here at the beginning of the dawn of a Day of Brahm. It is verily a beginning, for there is nothing to be seen—there is nothing but Space. No trace of Matter, Force or Mind, as we know these terms. In that portion of Infinite Space—that is, of course, in that "portion" of the Infinite Mind of the Absolute One, for even Space is a "conception" of that Mind, there is "Nothing." This is "the darkest moment, just before the dawn."

Then comes the breaking of the dawn of the Brahmic Day. The Absolute begins the "creation" of a Universe. And, how does It create? There can be no creation of something out of nothing. And except the Absolute Itself there is but Nothing.

Therefore The Absolute must create the Universe out of Its own "substance," if we can use the word "substance" in this connection. "Substance" means, literally, "that which stands under," being derived from the two Latin words, *sub,* meaning "under," and *stare,* meaning "to stand." The English word "understand" means, literally, "to stand under"—the two words really meaning the same. This is more than a coincidence.

So the Absolute must create the Universe from its own substance, we have seen. Well, what is this "substance" of the Absolute? Is it Matter? No! for Matter we know to be, in itself, merely a manifestation of Force, or Energy. Then, is it Force or Energy? No! because Force and Energy, in itself, cannot possess Mind, and we must think of the Absolute as possessing Mind, for it manifests Mind, and what is manifested must be in the Manifestor, or Manifesting Agent. Then this "substance" must be Mind? Well, yes, in a way—and yet not Mind as we know it, finite and imperfect. But something like Mind, only Infinite in degree and nature—something sufficiently greater than Mind as we know it, to admit of it being the Cause of Mind. But, we are compelled to think of it as "Infinite Mind," for our finite Minds can hold no higher conception. So we are content to say that this "substance" from which the Absolute must create the Universe is a something that we will call Infinite Mind. Fix this in your mind, please, as the first step in our conception.

But, how can the Infinite Mind be used to create finite minds, shapes, forms, and things, without it being lessened in quantity—how can you take something from something, and still have the original something left? An impossibility! And, we cannot think of the Absolute as "dividing Itself up" into two or more portions—for if such were the case, there would be two or more Absolutes, or else None. There cannot be two Absolutes, for if the Absolute were to divide itself so there would be no Absolute, but only two Relatives—two Finites instead of One Infinite. Do you see the absurdity?

Then how can this work of Creation be accomplished, in view of these difficulties which are apparent even to our finite minds? You may thresh this question over and over again in your minds—men have done so in all times—and you will not find the answer except in the fundamental Idea of the Yogi Teachings. And this Fundamental Idea is that the creation is purely a Mental Creation, and the Universe is the Mental Image, or Thought-Form, in the Mind of the Absolute—in the Infinite Mind, itself. No other "creation" is possible. And so this, say the Yogi Masters, this is the Secret of Universal Creation. The Universe is *of,* and *in,* the Infinite Mind, and this is the only way it could be so. So, fix in your mind this second step in our conception.

But then, you ask us, from whence comes Force, Matter, and Finite Mind? Well asked, good student—your answer shall be forthcoming. Here it is.

Finite Mind; Force or Energy; and Matter; in themselves have no existence. They are merely Mental Images, or Thought-Forms in the Infinite Mind of the Absolute. Their whole existence and appearance depends upon their Mental Conception and Retention in the Infinite Mind. In It they have their birth, rise, growth, decline and death.

Then what is Real about ME, you may ask—surely I have a vivid consciousness of Reality—is this merely an illusion, or shadow? No, not so! that sense of Reality which you possess and which every creature or thing possesses—that sense of "I Am"—is the perception by the Mental Image of the Reality of its Essence—and that Essence is the Spirit. And that Spirit is the SUBSTANCE OF THE ABSOLUTE embodied in Its conception, the Mental Image. It is the perception by the Finite, of its Infinite Essence. Or, the perception by the Relative of its Absolute Essence. Or, the perception by You, or I, or any other man or woman, of the Real Self, which underlies all the sham self or Personality. It is the reflection of the Sun, in the dew-drop, and thousands of dew-drops—seemingly thousands of Suns, and yet but One. And yet, that reflection of the Sun in the dew-drop is more than a "reflection," for it is the substance of the Sun itself—and yet the Sun shines on high, one and undivided, yet manifesting in millions of dew-drops. It is only by figures of speech that we can speak of the Unspeakable Reality.

To make it perhaps plainer to some of you, let us

remind you that even in your finite Mental Images there is evident many forms of life. You may think of a moving army of thousands of men. And yet the only "I" in these men is your own "I." These characters in your mind move and live and have their being, and yet there is nothing in them except "You!" The characters of Shakespeare, Dickens, Thackeray, Balzac, and the rest, were such strong Mental Images that not only their creators were carried away by their power, and apparent ability, but even you who read of them, many years after, perhaps, feel the apparent reality, and weep, or smile, or grow angry over their actions. And, yet there was no Hamlet, outside of Shakespeare's mind; no Micawber outside of Dickens; no Pere Goriot outside of Balzac.

These illustrations are but finite examples of the Infinite, but still they will give you an idea of the truth that we are trying to unfold in your mind. But you must not imagine that You and I, and all others, and things, are but mere "imaginations," like *our* created characters—that would be a most unhappy belief. The mental creations held by You and I, and other finite minds, are but *finite creations of finite minds,* while WE, ourselves, are the finite creations of an INFINITE MIND. While our, and Dickens', and Balzac's, and Shakespeare's creations live and move and have their being, they have no other "I" than our Finite Minds, while we, the characters in the Divine Drama, Story, or Epic, have for our "I"—our Real Self—the ABSOLUTE REALITY. They have merely a background of our finite personalities, and minds, before which they may desport themselves, until, alas! the very background fades away to dust, and both background and shadows disappear. But, we have behind our personalities the Eternal Background of Reality, which changeth not, neither doth it Disappear. Shadows on a screen though our Personalities may be, yet the Screen is Real and Eternal. Take away the finite screen and the shadows disappear—but our Screen remains forever.

We are Mental Images in the Infinite Mind—the Infinite Mind holds us safe—we cannot be lost—we cannot be hurt—we can never disappear, unless we be absorbed in the Infinite Mind itself, and then we STILL ARE! The Infinite Mind never forgets—it never can overlook us—it is aware of our presence, and being, always. We are safe—we are secure—we ARE! Just as we could not be created from Nothing—so we cannot be converted into Nothing. We are in the All—and there is no outside.

At the dawn of the Brahmic Day, The Absolute begins the creation of a new Universe, or the re-creation of one, just as you may care to state it. The highest Yogi Teachings inform us that the information relating to this event (which is, of course, beyond the personal knowledge of man as we know him) has been passed down to the race from teachers, who have received it from still higher teachers, and so on, and on and on, higher and higher, until it is believed to have originated with some of those wonderfully developed souls which have visited the earth from higher planes of Being, of which there are many. In these lessons we are making no claims of this sort, but pass on the teachings to you, believing that their truth will appeal to those who are ready for them, without any attempt to attribute to them an authority such as just mentioned. Our reference to this high source of the teachings was made because of its general acceptance in the Eastern countries, and by occultists generally.

The Yogi teachings inform us that, in the Beginning, The Absolute formed a Mental Image, or Thought-Form, of an Universal Mind—that is, of an Universal Principle of Mind. And here the distinction is made between this Universal Mind Principle, or Universal Mind-Stuff, as some have called it, and the Infinite Mind itself. The Infinite Mind is something infinitely above this creation of the Universal Mind Principle, the latter being as much an "emanation" as is Matter. Let there be no mistake about this. The Infinite Mind is Spirit—the Universal Mind Principle is "Mind-Stuff" of which all Finite Mind is a part. This Universal Mind Principle was the first conception of The Absolute, in the process of the creation of the Universe. It was the "Stuff" from which all Finite Mind forms, and is formed. It is the Universal Mental Energy. Know it as such—but do not confound it with Spirit, which we have called Infinite Mind, because we had no other term. There is a subtle difference here, which is most important to a careful understanding of the subject.

The Yogi teachings inform us that from this Mental Principle there was developed the Universal Principle of Force or Energy. And that from this Universal Force Principle there developed the Universal Principle of Matter. The Sanscrit terms for these Three Principles are as follows: *Chitta,* or the Universal Mind Substance, or Principle; *Prana,* or the Universal Energy Principle; and *Akasa,* or the Universal Principle of Matter. We have spoken of these Three Principles, or Three Great Manifestations, in our "Advanced Course" of lessons, which followed our "Fourteen Lessons," several years ago, but it becomes necessary for us to refer to them again at this place in connection with the present presentation of the subject. As was stated in the lessons just mentioned, these Three Manifestations, or Principles, are really one, and shade into each other. This matter has been fully touched upon in the concluding lessons of the aforesaid "Advanced Course," to which we must refer you for further details, in order to avoid repetition here. You will find a wonderful correspondence between these centuries-old Yogi teachings, and the latest conceptions of Modern Science.

Well, to return to the main path once more, the Teachings inform us that The Absolute "thought" into being—that is, held the Mental Image, or Thought-Form, of—*Chitta,* or Universal Mind Principle. This *Chitta* was finite, of course, and was bound and governed by the Laws of Finite Mind, imposed upon it by the Will of The Absolute. Everything that is Finite is governed by Laws imposed by the great LAW which we call The Absolute. Then began the Great INVOLUTION which was necessary before Evolution was possible. The word "Involve," you know, means "to wrap up; to cover; to hide; etc.;" and the word "Evolve" means "to unwrap; to unfold; to un-roll; etc." Before a thing can be "evolved," or "unfolded," it must first have been "involved" or "folded-in, or wrapped up, etc." Everything must be "involved" before it can be "evolved;" remember this, please—it is true on all planes, mental, physical, and spiritual. A thing must be "put in" before it may be "taken out." This truth, if remembered and applied to metaphysical problems, will throw the clearest light upon the darkest problems. Make it your own.

Therefore before the process of Evolution from the gross forms of Matter up to the higher, and then on to the Mental, from higher to higher, and then on the Spiritual plane—that Evolution which we see being performed before our sight today—before that Evolution became possible there was a necessary Involution, or "wrapping-up." The Spirit of the Absolute first "involved" itself in its Mental Image; Thought-Form, or Creation, of the Mind Principle, just as you may "involve" yourself in an earnest thought in deep meditation. Did you never "lose yourself" in thought, or "forget yourself" in an idea? Have you not spoken of yourself as having been "wrapped in thought?" Well, then you can see something of what is here meant, at least so far as the process of "involution" is concerned. You involve yourself in your meditations—the Absolute involves Itself in Its Mental Creations—but, remember the one is Finite, and the other Infinite, and the results are correspondingly weak or strong.

Obeying the laws imposed upon it, the Mental Principle then involved itself in the Energy Principle, or *Prana,* and the Universal Energy sprang into existence. Then, in obedience to the same Laws, the *Prana* involved itself in the *Akasa,* or Universal Matter Principle. Of course each "involving" practically "created" the "wrapper," "sheath" of the lower Principle. Do you see this? Each, therefore, depends upon the Principle higher than itself, which becomes its "Parent Principle," as the Yogis express it. And in this process of Involution the extreme form of Matter was reached before the process of Evolution became possible. The extreme form of gross Matter is not known to us today, on this planet, for we have passed beyond it. But the teachings inform us that such forms were as much grosser that the grossest Matter that we know today, as the latter is gross in comparison with the most ethereal vapors known to Modern Science. The human mind cannot grasp this extreme of the scale, any more than it can the extreme high degree of manifestation.

At this point we must call your attention to certain occult teachings, widely disseminated, which the highest Yogi teachers discountenance, and contradict. We allude to the teaching that in the process of Involution there was a "degeneration" or "devolution" from higher to lower forms of life, until the gross state of Matter was reached. Such a teaching is horrible, when considered in detail. It would mean that The Absolute deliberately created high forms of life, arch-angels, and higher than these—gods in fact—and then caused them to "devolve" until the lowest state was reached. This would mean the exact opposite of Evolution, and would mean a "going down" in accordance with the Divine Will, just as Evolution is a "going up" in accordance with the Divine Will.

This is contrary to man's best instincts, and the advanced Yogi teachings inform us that it is but an illusion or error that men have created by endeavoring to solve spiritual mysteries by purely intellectual processes. The true teaching is that the process of Involution was accomplished by a Principle involving itself in the lower Principle created within itself, and so on until the lowest plane was reached. Note the difference—"Principles as Principles" did this, and not as Individual Forms of Life or Being. There was no more a "devolution" in this process than there was in The Absolute involving itself in the Mental Image of the Mind Principle. There was no "devolution" or "going down"—only an "involution" or "wrapping up," of Principle, within Principle—the Individual Life not having as yet appeared, and not being possible of appearance until the Evolutionary process began.

We trust that we have made this point clear to you,

for it is an important matter. If the Absolute first made higher beings, and then caused them to "devolute" into lower and lower forms, then the whole process would be a cruel, purposeless thing, worthy only of some of the base conceptions of Deity conceived of by men in their ignorance. No! the whole effort of the Divine Will seems to be in the direction of "raising up" Individual Egos to higher and still higher forms. And in order to produce such Egos the process of "Involution" of Principles seems to have been caused, and the subsequent wonderful Evolutionary process instituted. What that "Reason" is, is Unknowable, as we have said over and over again. We cannot pry into the Infinite Mind of the Absolute, but we may form certain conclusions by observing and studying the Laws of the Universe, which seem to be moving in certain directions. From the manifested Will of the Divine One, we may at least hazard an idea as to its purposes. And these purposes seem to be always in an "upward" lifting and evolution. Even the coming of the "Night of Brahm" is no exception to this statement, as we shall see in future lessons.

From the starting of the process of Involution from the Mental Principle, down to the extreme downward point of the grossest Manifestation of Matter, there were many stages. From the highest degree of the Finite Mind, down to lower and still lower degrees; then on to the plane of Force and Energy, from higher to lower degrees of Principle within Principle; then on to the plane of Matter, the Involutionary urge proceeded to work. When the plane of Matter was reached, it, of course, showed its highest degree of manifested Matter—the most subtle form of Ether, or *Akasa.* Then down, down, down, went the degrees of Matter, until the grossest possible form was reached, and then there was a moment's pause, before the Evolutionary process, or upward-movement, began. The impulse of the Original Will, or Thought, had exhausted its downward urge, and now began the upward urge or tendency. But here was manifested a new feature.

This new feature was "The Tendency toward Individualization." During the downward trend the movement was *en masse,* that is, by Principle *as Principle,* without any "splitting up" into portions, or centers. But with the first upward movement there was evidenced a tendency toward creating Centers of Energy, or Units of activity, which then manifested itself, as the evolutionary movement continued, from electrons to atoms; from atoms to man. The gross matter was used as material for the formation of finer and more complex forms; and these in turn combined, and formed higher, and so on, and on. And the forms of Energy operated in the same way. And the manifestations of centers of Mind or consciousness in the same way. But all in connection. Matter, Energy and Mind formed a Trinity of Principles, and worked in connection. And the work was always in the direction of causing higher and higher "forms" to arise—higher and higher Units—higher and higher Centers. But in every form, center or unit, there was manifested the Three Principles, Mind, Energy, and Matter. And within each was the ever present Spirit. For Spirit *must* be in All—just as All must be in Spirit.

And, so this Evolutionary process has continued ever since ,and must continue for aeons yet. The Absolute is raising itself up into Itself higher and higher Egos, and is providing them with higher and higher sheaths in which to manifest. And, as we shall see in these lessons, as we progress, this evolution is not only along the physical lines, but also along the mental. And it concerns itself not only with "bodies," but with "souls," which also evolve, from time to time, and bodies are given these souls in order that they may work out their evolution. And the whole end and aim of it all seems to be that Egos may reach the stage where they are conscious of the Real Self—of the Spirit within them, and its relation to the Spirit of the Absolute, and then go on and on and on, to planes of life and being, and activities of which even the most advanced of the race may only dream.

As some of the Ancient Yogi Teachers have said: "Men are evolving into super-men; and super-men into gods; and gods into super-gods; and super-gods into Something still higher; until from the lowest bit of matter enclosing life, unto the highest being—yea, even unto The Absolute—there is an Infinite Ladder of Being—and yet the One Spirit pervades all; is in all, as the all is in It."

The Creative Will, of which we have spoken in these

lessons, is in full operation all through Life. The Natural Laws are laws of Life imposed by The Absolute in his Mental Image. They are the Natural Laws of this Universe, just as other Universes have other Laws. But The Absolute Itself has no Laws affecting It—It, in Itself *is* LAW.

And these Laws of Life, and Nature, along its varying planes, Material, of Energy; and Mental; are also, in the Divine Mind, else they would not be at all, even in appearance. And when they are transcended, or apparently defied by some man of advanced development, it is only because such a man is able to rise above the plane upon which such laws are operative. But even this transcending is, in itself, in accordance with some higher law.

And so, we see that All, high and low—good and bad—simple or complex—all are contained Within the Mind of the One. Gods, angels, adepts, sages, heavens, planes,—all, everything—is within the Universe, and the Universe is Within the Mind of the One. And all is proceeding in accordance with Law. And all is moving upward and onward, along the lines of Evolution. All is Well. We are held firmly in The Mind of the One.

And, just as the tendency was from the general Principle toward the particular Individual Soul, so is there a Reconciliation later on, for the Individual soul, as it develops and unfolds, loses its sense of Separateness, and begins to feel its identity with the One Spirit, and moves along the lines of unfoldment, until it becomes in Conscious Union with God. Spiritual Evolution does not mean the "growth of the Spirit," for the Spirit cannot grow—it is already Perfect. The term means the unfoldment of the Individual Mind, until it can recognize the Spirit Within.

Let us close this lesson with the

CENTRAL THOUGHT.

There is but ONE. That ONE is Spirit. In the Infinite Mind of that ONE SPIRIT there arose the Mental Image or Thought-Form of this Universe. Beginning with the Thought of the Principle in Mind; and passing on to the Principle of Energy; and then on to the Principle of Matter; proceeded the Involutionary Process of Creation. Then, upward began the Evolutionary Process, and Individual Centers or Units were formed. And the tendency, and evolutionary urge is ever in the direction of "unfolding" within the Ego of the Realization of the Indwelling Spirit. As we throw off sheath after sheath, we approach nearer and nearer to the SPIRIT within us, which is the One Spirit pervading all things. This is the Meaning of Life—the Secret of Evolution. All the Universe is contained Within the Mind of The One. There is Nothing outside of that Infinite Mind. There is no Outside, for the One is All in All; Space, Time, and Laws, being but Mental Images in that Mind, as are likewise all shapes and forms, and phenomena. And as the Ego unfolds into a realization of Itself—Its

Real Self—so does its Wisdom and Power expand. It thus enters into a greater and greater degree of its Inheritance. Within the Mind of the One, is All there is. And I, and Thou, and All Things are HERE within that Infinite Mind. We are always "held in Mind" by The Absolute—are always safe here. There is nothing to harm us, in Reality, for our Real Self is the Real Self of the Infinite Mind. All is Within the Mind of the One. Even the tiniest atom is under the Law, and protected by the Law. And the LAW is All there Is. And in that Law we may rest Content and Unafraid. May this Realization be YOURS.

PEACE BE WITH YOU ALL.

THE SEVENTH LESSON

Cosmic Evolution.

We have now reached a most interesting point in this course of lessons, and a period of fascinating study lies before us from now until the close of the course. We have acquainted ourselves with the fundamental principles, and will now proceed to witness these principles in active operation. We have studied the Yogi Teachings concerning the Truth underlying all things, and shall now pass on to a consideration of the process of Cosmic Evolution; the Cyclic Laws; the Law of Spiritual Evolution, or Reincarnation; the Law of Spiritual Cause and Effect, or *Karma;* etc. In this lesson we begin the story of the upward progress of the Universe, and its forms, shapes, and forces, from the point of the "moment's pause" following the ceasing of the process of Involution—the point at which Cosmic Evolution begins. Our progress is now steadily upward, so far as the evolution of Individual Centres is concerned. We shall see the principles returning to the Principle—the centres returning to the great Centre from which they emanated during the process of Involution. We shall study the long. gradual, but steady ascent of Man, in his journey toward god-hood. We shall see the Building of an Universe, and the Growth of the Soul.

In our last lesson we have seen that at the dawn of a Brahmic Day, the Absolute begins the creation of a new Universe. The Teachings inform us that in the beginning, the Absolute forms a Mental Image, or

Thought-Form of an Universal Mind Principle, or Universal Mind-Stuff, as some of the teachers express it. Then this Universal Mind Principle creates within itself the Universal Energy Principle. Then this Universal Energy Principle creates within itself the Universal Matter Principle. Thus, Energy is a product of Mind; and Matter a product of Energy.

The Teachings then further inform us that from the rare, tenuous, subtle form of Matter in which the Universal Matter Principle first appeared, there was produced forms of Matter less rare; and so by easy stages, and degrees, there appeared grosser and still grosser forms of matter, until finally there could be no further involution into grosser forms, and the Involutionary Process ceased. Then ensued the "moment's pause" of which the Yogi teachers tell us. At that point Matter existed as much grosser that the grossest form of Matter now known to us, as the latter is when compared to the most subtle vapors known to science. It is impossible to describe these lower forms of matter, for they have ages since disappeared from view, and we would have no words with which to describe them. We can understand the situation only by comparisons similar to the above.

Succeeding the moment's pause, there began the Evolutionary Process, or Cosmic Evolution, which has gone on ever since, and which will go on for ages to come. From the grossest forms of Matter there evolved forms a little more refined, and so on and on. From the simple elementary forms, evolved more complex and intricate forms. And from these forms combinations began to be formed. And the urge was ever upward.

But remember this, that all of this Evolutionary Process is but a Returning Home. It is the Ascent after the Descent. It is not a Creation but an Unfoldment. The Descent was made by principles as principles—the Ascent is being made by Individualized Centres evolved from the principles. Matter manifests finer and finer forms, and exhibits a greater and greater subservience to Energy or Force. And Energy or Force shows a greater and greater degree of "mind" in it. But, remember this, that there is Mind in even the grossest form of Matter. This must be so, for what springs from a thing must contain the elements of its cause.

And the Cosmic Evolution continues, and must continue for aeons of time. Higher and higher forms of Mind are being manifested, and still higher and higher forms will appear in the scale, as the process continues. The evolution is not only along material lines, but has passed on to the mental planes, and is now operating along the spiritual lines as well. And the end, and aim seems to be that each Ego, after the experiences of many lives, may unfold and develop to a point where it may become conscious of its Real Self, and realize its identity with the One Life, and the Spirit.

At this point we may be confronted with the objection of the student of material science, who will ask why we begin our consideration of Cosmic Evolution at a point in which matter has reached the limit of its lowest vibrations, manifesting in the grossest possible form of matter. These students may point to the fact that Science begins its consideration of evolution with the *nebulae,* or faint cloudlike, vaporous matter, from which the planets were formed. But there is only an apparent contradiction here. The *nebulae* were part of the Process of Involution, and Science is right when it holds that the gross forms were produced from the finer. But the process of change from finer to grosser was *Involution,* not Evolution. Do you see the difference? Evolution begins at the point when the stage of Unfoldment commenced. When the gross forms begin to yield to the new upward urge, and unfold into finer forms—then begins Evolution.

We shall pass over the period of Evolution in which Matter was evolving into finer and still finer forms, until at last it reached a degree of vibration capable of supporting that which we call "life." Of course there is "life" in all matter—even in the atom, as we have shown in previous lessons. But when we speak of "life," as we now do, we mean what are generally called "living forms." The Yogi Teachings inform us that the lowest forms of what we call "life" were evolved from forms of high crystal life, which indeed they very much resemble. We have spoken of this resemblance, in the previous lessons of this series. And, so we shall begin at the point where "living forms" began.

Speaking now of our own planet, the Earth, we find matter emerging from the molten state in which it manifested for ages. Gradually cooling and stratifying, the Earth contained none of those forms that we call living forms. The temperature of the Earth in that period is estimated at about 15,000 times hotter than boiling water, which would, of course, render impossible the existence of any of the present known forms of life. But the Yogi Teachings inform us that even in the molten mass there were elementary forms that were to become the ancestral forms of the later living forms. These elementary forms were composed of a vaporous, peculiar form of matter, of minute size,—little more than the atoms, in fact, and yet, just a little more advanced. From these elementary forms, there gradually evolved, as the Earth cooled and solidified, other forms, and so on until at last the first "living form" manifested.

As the globe cooled at the poles, there was gradually created a tropical climate, in which the temperature was sufficiently cool to support certain rudimentary forms of life. In the rocks in the far northern latitudes, there are found abundant traces of fossils, which goes to prove the correctness of the Yogi Teachings of the origin of life at the north pole, from which the living forms gradually spread south toward the equator, as the Earth's surface cooled.

The elementary evolving life forms were of a very simple structure, and were but a degree above the crystals. They were composed of identically the same substance as the crystals, *the only difference being that they displayed a greater degree of mind.* For that matter, even the highest physical form known to us today is composed of simple chemical materials. And these chemical materials are obtained, either directly or indirectly, from the air, water, or earth. The principal materials composing the physical bodies of plants, animals, and man, are oxygen, carbon, hydrogen, nitrogen, with a still smaller proportion of sulphur and phosphorus, and traces of a few other elements. The material part of all living things is alike—the difference lies in the degree of Mind controlling the matter in which it is embodied.

Of these physical materials, carbon is the most important to the living forms. It seems to possess properties capable of drawing to it the other elements, and forcing them into service. From carbon proceeds what is called "protoplasm," the material of which the cells of animal and vegetable life is composed. From protoplasm the almost infinite varieties of living forms have been built up by the process of Evolution, working gradually and by easy stages. Every living form is made up, or composed, of a multitude of single cells, and their combinations. And every form originates in a single cell which rapidly multiplies and reproduces itself until the form of the amoeba; the plant; the animal; the man, is completed. All living forms are but a single cell multiplied. And every cell is composed of protoplasm. Therefore we must look for the beginning of life in the grade of matter called protoplasm. In this both modern Science and the Yogi Teachings agree fully.

In investigating protoplasm we are made to realize the wonderful qualities of its principal constituent—Carbon. Carbon is the wonder worker of the elements. Manifesting in various forms, as the diamond, graphite, coal, protoplasm—is it not entitled to respect? The Yogi Teachings inform us that in Carbon we have that form of matter which was evolved as the physical basis of life. If any of you doubt that inorganic matter may be transformed into living forms, let us refer you to the plant life, in which you may see the plants building up cells every day from the inorganic, chemical or mineral substances, in the earth, air, and water. Nature performs every day the miracle of transforming chemicals and minerals into living plant cells. And when animal or man eats these plant cells, so produced, they become transformed into animal cells of which the body is built up. What it took Nature ages to do in the beginning, is now performed in a few hours, or minutes.

The Yogi Teachings, again on all-fours with modern Science, inform us that living forms had their beginning in water. In the slimy bed of the polar seas the simple cell-forms appeared, having their origin in the transitional stages before mentioned. The first living forms were a lowly form of plant life, consisting of a single cell. From these forms were evolved forms composed of groups of cells, and so proceeded the work of evolution, from the lower form to the higher, ever in an upward path.

As we have said, the single cell is the physical centre, or parent, of every living form. It contains what is known as the *nucleus,* or kernel, which seems to be more highly organized than the rest of the material of the cell—it may be considered as the "brain" of the cell, if you wish to use your imagination a little. The single cell reproduces itself by growth and division, or separation. Each cell manifests the functions of life, whether it be a single-celled creature, or a cell which with billions of others, goes to make up a higher form. It feels, feeds, grows, and reproduces itself. In the single-celled creature, the one cell performs all of the functions, of course. But as the forms become more complex, the many cells composing a form perform certain functions which are allotted to it, the division of labor resulting in a higher manifestation. This is true not only in the case of animal forms, but also in the case of plant forms. The cells in the bone, muscle, nerve-tissue and blood of the animal differ according to their offices; and the same is true in the cells in the sap, stem, root, leaf, seed and flower of the plant.

As we have said, the cells multiply by division, after a period of growth. The cell grows by material taken into its substance, as food. When sufficient food has been partaken, and enough new material accumulated to cause the cell to attain a certain size, then it divides, or separates into two cells, the division being equal, and the point of cleavage being at the kernel or nucleus. As the two parts separate, the protoplasm of each groups itself around its nucleus, and two living forms exist where there was but one a moment before. And then each of the two cells proceed to grow rapidly, and then separate, and so on to the end, each cell multiplying into millions, as time passes.

Ascending in the scale, we next find the living forms composed of cell-groups. These cell-groups are formed by single cells dividing, and then subdividing, but instead of passing on their way they group themselves in clusters, or masses. There are millions of forms of these cell-group creatures, among which we find the sponges, polyps, etc.

In the early forms of life it is difficult to distinguish between the animal and the plant forms, in fact the early forms partake of the qualities of both. But as we advance in the scale a little there is seen a decided "branching out," and one large branch is formed of the evolving plant forms, and the other of the evolving animal forms. The plant-branch begins with the sea-weeds, and passes on to the fungi, lichens, mosses, ferns, pines and palm-ferns, grasses, etc., then to the trees, shrubs and herbs. The animal-branch begins with the *monera,* or single-cell forms, which are little more than a drop of sticky, glue-like protoplasm. Then it passes on to the *amoebae,* which begins to show a slight difference in its parts. Then on the *foraminifera,* which secretes a shell of lime from the water. Then on a step higher to the *polycystina,* which secretes a shell, or skeleton of flint-like material from the water. Then come the sponges. Then the coral-animals, anemones and jelly-fish. Then come the sea-lilies, star-fish, etc. Then the various families of worms. Then the crabs, spiders, centipedes, insects. Then come the mollusca, which include the oysters, clams and other shell-fish; snails, cuttle-fish, sea-squirts, etc. All of the above families of animal-forms are what are known as "invertebrates," that is, without a backbone.

Then we come to the "vertebrates," or animals having a backbone. First we see the fish family with its thousands of forms. Then come the amphibia, which include the toads, frogs, etc. Then come the reptiles, which include the serpents, lizards, crocodiles, turtles, etc. Then come the great family of birds, with its wonderful variety of forms, sizes, and characteristics. Then come the mammals, the name of which comes from the Latin word meaning "the breast," the characteristic of which group comes from the fact that they nourish their young by milk, or similar fluid, secreted by the mother. The mammals are the highest form of the vertebrates.

First among the mammals we find the aplacentals, or those which bring forth immature young, which are grouped into two divisions, *i. e.,* (1) the *monotremes,* or one-vented animals, in which group belong the duck-bills, spiny ant-eaters, etc.; and (2) the *marsupials,* or pouched animals, in which group belong the kangaroo, opossum, etc.

The next highest form among the mammals are known as the *placentals,* or those which bring forth mature young. In this class are found the ant-eaters, sloth, manatee, the whale and porpoise, the horse, cow, sheep, and other hoofed animals; the elephant, seal, the dog, wolf, lion, tiger, and all flesh eating animals; the hares, rats, mice, and all other gnawing animals; the bats, moles, and other insect-feeders; then come the great family of apes, from the small monkeys up to the orang-outang, chimpanzee, and other forms nearly approaching man. And then comes the highest, Man, from the Kaffir, Bush-man, Cave-man, and Digger Indian, up through the many stages until the highest forms of our own race are reached.

From the Monera to Man is a long path, containing many stages, but it is a path including all the intermediate forms. The Yogi Teachings hold to the theory of evolution, as maintained by modern Science, but it goes still further, for it holds not only that the physical forms are subject to the evolutionary process, but that also the "souls" embodied in these forms are subject to the evolutionary process. In other words the Yogi Teachings hold that there is a twin-process of evolution under way, the main object of which is to develop "souls," but which also finds it necessary to evolve higher and higher forms of physical bodies for these constantly advancing souls to occupy.

Let us take a hasty glance at the ascending forms of animal life, as they rise in the evolutionary scale. By so doing we can witness the growth of the soul, within them, as manifested by the higher and higher physical forms which are used as channels of expression by the souls within. Let us first study soul-evolution from the outer viewpoint, before we proceed to examine it from the inner. By so doing we will have a fuller idea of the process than if we ignored the outer and proceed at once to the inner. Despise not the outer form, for it has always been, and is now, the Temple of the Soul, which the latter is remodelling and rebuilding in order to accommodate its constantly increasing needs and demands.

Let us begin with the *Protozoa,* or one-celled forms—the lowest form of animal life. The lowest form of this lowest class is that remarkable creature that we have mentioned in previous lessons—the *Moneron.* This creature lives in water, the natural element in which organic life is believed to have had its beginning. It is a very tiny, shapeless, colorless, slimy, sticky mass—something like a tiny drop of glue—alike all over and in its mass, and without organs or parts of any kind. Some have claimed that below the field of the microscope there may be something like elementary organs in the Moneron, but so far as the human eye may discover there is no evidence of anything of the kind. It has no organs or parts with which to perform particular functions, as is the case with the higher forms of life. These functions, as you know, may be classed into three groups, *i. e.,* nutrition, reproduction, and relation—that is, the function of feeding, the function of reproducing its kind, and the function of receiving and responding to the impressions of the outside world. All of these three classes of functions the Moneron performs—but *with any part of its body, or with all of it.*

Every part, or the whole, of the Moneron absorbs food and oxygen—it is all mouth and lungs. Every part, or the whole, digests the food—it is all stomach. Every part, or the whole, performs the reproductive function—it is all reproductive organism. Every part of it senses the impressions from outside, and responds to it—it is all organs of sense, and organs of motion. It envelops its prey as a drop of glue surrounds a particle of sand, and then absorbs the substance of the prey into its own substance. It moves by prolonging any part of itself outward in a sort of tail-like appendage, which it uses as a "foot," or "finger" with which to propel itself; draw itself to, or push itself away from an object. This prolongation is called a *pseudopod,* or "false-foot." When it gets through using the "false-foot" for the particular purpose, it simply draws back into itself that portion which had been protruded for the purpose.

It performs the functions of digestion, assimilation, elimination, etc., perfectly, just as the higher forms of life—but it has no organs for the functions, and performs them severally, and collectively with any, or all parts of its body. What the higher animals perform with intricate organs and parts—heart, stomach, lungs, liver, kidneys, etc., etc.—this tiny creature performs *without organs,* and with its entire body, or any part thereof. The function of reproduction is startlingly simple in the case of the Moneron. It simply divides itself in two parts, and that is all there is to it. There is no male or female sex in its case—it combines both within itself. The reproductive process is even far more simple than the "budding" of plants. You may turn one of these wonderful creatures inside out, and still it goes on the even tenor of its way, in no manner disturbed or affected. It is simply a "living drop of glue," which eats, digests, receives impressions and responds thereto, and reproduces itself. This tiny glue-drop performs virtually the same life functions as do the higher complex forms of living things. Which is the greater "miracle"—the Moneron or Man?

A slight step upward from the Moneron brings us to the *Amoeba*. The name of this new creature is derived from the Greek word meaning "change," and has been bestowed because the creature is constantly changing its shape. This continual change of shape is caused by a continuous prolongation and drawing-in of its pseudopods, or "false-feet," which also gives the creature the appearance of a "many-fingered" organism. This creature shows the first step toward "parts," for it has something like a membrane or "skin" at its surface, and a "nucleus" at its centre, and also an expanding and contracting cavity within its substance, which it uses for holding, digesting and distributing its food, and also for storing and distributing its oxygen—an elementary combination of stomach and lungs! So you see that the amoeba has taken a step upward from the moneron, and is beginning to appreciate the convenience of parts and organs. It is interesting to note, in this connection, that while the ordinary cells of the higher animal body resemble the *monera* in many ways, still the white corpuscles in the blood of man and the animals bear a startling resemblance to the *amoebae* so far as regards size, general structure, and movements, and are in fact known to Science as "amoeboids." The white corpuscles change their shape, take in food in an intelligent manner, and live a comparatively independent life, their movements showing independent "thought" and "will."

Some of the amoebae (the diatoms, for instance) secrete solid matter from the water, and build therefrom shells or houses, which serve to protect them from their enemies. These shells are full of tiny holes, through which the pseudopods are extended in their search for food, and for purposes of movement. Some of these shells are composed of secreted lime, and others of a flinty substance, the "selection" of these substances from the other mineral particles in the water, evidencing a degree of "thought," and mind, even in these lowly creatures. The skeletons of these tiny creatures form vast deposits of chalk and similar substances.

Next higher in the scale are the *Infusoria.* These creatures differ from the amoebae inasmuch as instead of pseudopods, they have developed tiny vibrating filaments, or thread-like appendages, which are used for drawing in their prey and for moving about. These filaments are permanent, and are not temporary like the pseudopods of the monera or amoebae—they are the *first signs of permanent hands and feet.* These creatures have also discovered the possibilities of organs and parts, to a still greater degree than have their cousins the amoebae, and have evolved something like a mouth-opening (very rudimentary) and also a short gullet through which they pass their food and oxygen —*they have developed the first signs of a throat, windpipe and food-passage.*

Next come the family of Sponges, the soft skeletons of which form the useful article of everyday use. There are many forms who weave a home of far more delicacy and beauty than their more familiar and homely brothers. The sponge creature itself is a slimy, soft creature, which fills in the spaces in its spongy skeleton. It is fastened to one spot, and gathers in its food from the water around it (and oxygen as well), by means of numerous whip-like filaments called *cilia,* which flash through the water driving in the food and oxygen to the inner positions of its body. The water thus drawn in, as well as the refuse from the food, is then driven out in the same manner. It is interesting to note that in the organisms of the higher animals, including man, there are numerous *cilia* performing offices in connection with nutrition, etc. When Nature perfects an instrument, it is very apt to retain it, even in the higher forms, although in the latter its importance may be dwarfed by higher ones.

The next step in the ascending scale of life-forms is

occupied by the *polyps,* which are found in water, fastened to floating matter. The polyps fasten themselves to this floating matter, with their mouths downward, from the latter dangling certain tentacles, or thin, long arms. These tentacles contain small thread-like coils in contact with a poisonous fluid, and enclosed in a cell. When the tentacles come in contact with the prey of the creature, or with anything that is sensed as a possible enemy, they contract around the object and the little cells burst and the tiny thread-like coils are released and twist themselves like a loop around the object, poisoning it with the secreted fluid. Some of the polyps secrete flint-like tubes, which they inhabit, and from the ends of which they emerge like flowers. From these parent polyps emerge clusters of young, resembling buds. These bud-like young afterwards become what are known as jelly-fishes, etc., which in turn reproduce themselves—but here is a wonder—the jelly-fish lay eggs, which when hatched produce stationary polyps like their grandparent, and not moving creatures like their parents. The jelly-fishes have a comparatively complex organism. They have an intricate system of canal-like passages with which to convey their food and oxygen to the various parts. They also have something like muscles, which contract and enable the creature to "swim." They also possess a "nervous system," and, most wonderful of all, they have *rudimentary eyes and ears.* Their tentacles, like those of the parent-polyp, secrete the poisonous fluid which is discharged into prey or enemy.

Akin to the polyps are the sea-anemones, with their beautiful colors, and still more complex structure and organism, the tentacles of which resemble the petals of a flower. Varying slightly from these are the coral-creatures, which form in colonies and the skeletons of which form the coral trees and branches, and other forms, with which we are familiar.

Passing on to the next highest family of life-forms, we see the spiny-bodied sea-creatures, such as the sea-urchin, star-fish, etc., which possess a thick, hard skin, covered by spines or prickly projections. These creatures abound in numerous species. The star-fish has rays projecting from a common centre, which gives it its name, while the sea-urchin resembles a ball. The sea-lilies, with their stems and flowers (so-called) belong to this family, as do also the sea-cucumbers, whose name is obtained from their shape and general appearance, but which are animals possessing a comparatively complex organism, one of the features of which is a stomach which may be discarded at will and replaced by a new one. These creatures have a well defined nervous system, and have eyes, and some of them even rudimentary eyelids.

Ascending the scale of life-forms, we next observe the great family of the *Annulosa,* or jointed creatures, which comprises the various families of the worm, the crab, the spider, the ant, etc. In this great family are grouped nearly four-fifths of the known life-forms. Their bodies are well formed and they have nervous systems running along the body and consisting of two thin threads, knotted at different points into ganglia or masses of nerve cells similar to those possessed by the higher animals. They possess eyes and other sense organs, in some cases highly developed. They possess organs, corresponding to the heart, and have a well-developed digestive apparatus. Note this advance in the nutritive organism: the *moneron* takes its food at any point of its body; the *amoeba* takes its food by means of its "false-feet," and drives it through its body by a rhythmic movement of its substance; the *polyp* distributes its food to its various parts by means of the water which it absorbs with the food; the *sea-urchin and star-fish* distribute their food by canals in their bodies which open directly into the water; in the higher forms of the *annulosa,* the food is distributed by a fluid resembling blood, which carries the nourishment to every part and organ, and which carries away the waste matter, the blood being propelled through the body by a rudimentary heart. The oxygen is distributed by each of these forms in a corresponding way, the higher forms having rudimentary lungs and respiratory organs. Step by step the life-forms are perfected, and the organs necessary to perform certain definite functions are evolved from rudimentary to perfected forms.

The families of worms are the humblest members of the great family of the Annulosa. Next come the creatures called Rotifers, which are very minute. Then come the Crustacea, so called from their crustlike shell. This group includes the crabs, lobsters, etc., and closely resembles the insects. In fact, some of the best authorities believe that the insects and the crustacea spring from the same parent form, and some of the Yogi authorities hold to this belief, while others do not attempt to pass upon it, deeming it immaterial, inasmuch as all life-forms have a common origin. The western scientists pay great attention to outward details, while the Oriental mind is apt to pass over these details as of slight importance, preferring to seek the cause back of the outward form. On one point both the Yogi teachers and the scientists absolutely agree, and that is that the family of insect life had its origin in some aquatic creature. Both hold that the wings of the insect have been evolved from organs primarily used for breathing purposes by the ancestor when it took short aerial flights, the need for means of flight afterwards acting to develop these rudimentary organs into perfected wings. There need be no more wonder expressed at this change than in the case of the transformation of the insect from grub to chrysalis, and then to insect. In fact this process is a reproduction of the stages through which the life-form passed during the long ages between sea-creature and land-insect.

We need not take up much of your time in speaking of the wonderful complex organism of some of the insect family, which are next on the scale above the crustacea. The wonders of spider-life—the almost human life of the ants—the spirit of the beehive—and all the rest of the wonders of insect life are familiar to all of our readers. A study of some good book on the life of the higher forms of the insect family will prove of value to anyone, for it will open his or her eyes to the wonderful manifestation of life and mind among these creatures. Remember the remark of Darwin, that the brain of the ant, although not much larger than a pin point, "is one of the most marvelous atoms of matter in the world, perhaps more so than the brain of man."

Closely allied to the crustacea is the sub-family of the *mollusca,* which includes the oyster, clams, and similar creatures; also the snails, cuttle-fish, slugs, nautilus, sea-squirts, etc., etc. Some are protected by a hard shell, while others have a gristly outer skin, serving as an armor, while others still are naked. Those having shells secrete the material for their construction from the water. Some of them are fixed to rocks, etc., while others roam at will. Strange as it may appear at first sight, some of the higher forms of the mollusca show signs of a rudimentary vertebra, and science has hazarded the opinion that the sea-squirts and similar creatures were descended from some ancestor from whom also descended the vertebrate animals, of which man is the highest form known today on this planet. We shall mention this connection in our next lesson, where we will take up the story of "The Ascent of Man" from the lowly vertebrate forms.

And now, in closing this lesson, we must remind

the reader that we are *not* teaching Evolution as it is conceived by modern science. We are viewing it from the opposite viewpoint of the Yogi Teaching. Modern Science teaches that Mind is a by-product of the evolving material forms—while the Yogi Teachings hold that there was Mind *involved* in the lowest form, and that that Mind constantly pressing forward for unfoldment *compelled* the gradual evolution, or unfoldment of the slowly advancing degrees of organization and function. Science teaches that "function precedes organization," that is, that a form performs certain functions, imperfectly and crudely, before it evolves the organs suitable for the functioning. For instance the lower forms digested food before they evolved stomachs—the latter coming to meet the need. But the Yogi Teachings go further and claim that "desire precedes function," that is, that the lowly life form "desires" to have digestive apparatus, in order to proceed in the evolutionary scale, before it begins the functioning that brings about the more complex organism. There is ever the "urge" of the Mind which craves unfoldment, and which the creatrue feels as a dim desire, which grows stronger and stronger as time goes on. Some yield more readily to the urge, and such become the parents of possible higher forms. "Many are called, but few are chosen," and so matters move along slowly from generation to generation, a few forms serving to carry on the evolutionary urge to their descendants. But is always the Evolutionary Urge of the imprisoned Mind striving to cast aside its sheaths and to have more perfect machinery with which, and through which, to manifest and express itself? This is the difference between the "Evolution" of Modern Science and the "Unfoldment" of the Yogi Teachings. The one is all material, with mind as a mere by-product, while the other is all Mind, with matter as a tool and instrument of expression and manifestation.

As we have said in this lesson—and as we shall point out to you in detail in future lessons—accompanying this evolution of bodies there is an evolution of "souls" producing the former. This evolution of souls is a basic principle of the Yogi Teachings, but it is first necessary that you acquaint yourselves with the evolution of bodies and forms, before you may fully grasp the higher teachings.

Our next lesson will be entitled "The Ascent of Man," in which the rise of man—that is, his body—from the lowly forms of the vertebrates is shown. In the same lesson we shall begin our consideration of the "evolution of souls." We trust that the students are carefully studying the details of each lesson, for every lesson has its part in the grand whole of the Teachings.

THE EIGHTH LESSON

The Ascent of Man.

In our last lesson we led you by successive steps from the beginnings of Life in living forms up to the creatures closely resembling the family of vertebrates—the highest family of living forms on this planet. In this present lesson we take up the story of the "Ascent of Man" from the lowly vertebrate forms.

The large sub-family of forms called "The Vertebrates" are distinguished from the Invertebrates by reason of the former possessing an *internal* bony skeleton, the most important feature of which is the vertebra or spinal column. The vertebrates, be it remembered, possess practically the same organs as the lower forms of life, but differ from them most materially by the possession of the *internal* skeleton, the lower forms having an *external* or outside *skeleton,* which latter is merely a hardening of the skin.

The flexibility of the vertebra creates a wonderful strength of structure, combined with an ease of movement peculiar to the vertebrates, and which renders them the natural forms of life capable of rapid development and evolution. By means of this strength, and ease, these forms are enabled to move rapidly in pursuit of their prey, and away from their pursuers, and also to resist outside pressure or attack. They are protected in a way similar to the invertebrates having shells, and yet have the additional advantage of easy movement. Differing in shape and appearance as do the numerous members of the sub-family of vertebrates, still their structure is easily seen to spring from a single form—all are modifications of some common pattern, the differences arising from the necessities of the life of the animal, as manifested through the desire and necessities of the species.

Science shows the direct relationship between the Vertebrates, and the Invertebrates by means of several connecting-links, the most noticeable of which is the Lancelot, a creature resembling the fish-form, and yet also closely resembling the lower (invertebrate) forms of life. This creature has no head, and but one eye. It is semi-transparent, and possesses *cilia* for forcing in the water containing its food. It has something like gills, and a gullet like the lower forms. It has no heart, the blood being circulated by means of contracting vessels or parts. Strictly speaking, it has no back-bone, or vertebra, but still Science has been compelled to class it among the vertebrates because is has a gristly cartilage where the back-bone is found in the higher forms. This gristle may be called an "elementary spine." It has a nervous system consisting of a single cord which spreads into a broadened end near the creature's mouth, and which may therefore be regarded as "something like a brain." This creature is really a developed form of Invertebrate, shaped like a Vertebrate, and showing signs of a rudimentary spine and nervous system of the latter. It is a "connecting-link."

The lowest forms of the true Vertebrates are the

great families of Fishes. These Fish families include fishes of high and low degree, some of the higher forms being as different from the lowest as they (the highest) are different from the Reptile family. It is not necessary to go into detail regarding the nature of the fish families, for every student is more or less familiar with them.

Some peculiar forms of fish show a shading into the Reptile family, in fact they seem to belong nearly as much to the latter as to their own general family. Some species of fish known as the *Dipnoi* or "double-breathers," have a remarkable dual system of breathing. That is, they have gills for breathing while in the water, and also have a primitive or elementary "lung" in the shape of an air-bladder, or "sound," which they use for breathing on land. The Mud-fish of South America, and also other forms in Australia and other places, have a modification of fins which are practically "limbs," which they actually use for traveling on land from pond to pond. Some of these fish have been known to travel enormous distances in search of new pools of water, or new streams, having been driven from their original homes by droughts, or perhaps by instincts similar to the migrating instinct of birds. Eels are *fish* (although many commonly forget this fact) and many of their species are able to leave the water and travel on land from pond to pond, their breathing being performed by a peculiar modification of the gills. The climbing perch of India are able to live out of water, and have modified gills for breathing purposes, and modified fins for climbing and walking. So you see that without leaving the fish family proper, we have examples of land-living creatures which are akin to "connecting links."

But there are real "connecting-links" between the Fish and the Reptiles. Passing over the many queer forms which serve as links between the two families, we have but to consider our common frog's history for a striking example. The Tadpole has gills, has no limbs, uses its tail like a fish's fin, eats plants, etc. Passing through several interesting stages the Tadpole reaches a stage in which it is a frog with a tail—then it sheds its tail and is a full fledged Frog, with four legs; web-feet; no tail; and feeding on animals. The Frog is amphibious, that is, able to live on land or in water—and yet it is compelled to come to the surface of the water for air to supply its lungs. Some of the amphibious animals possess both lungs and gills, even when matured; but the higher vertebrates living in the water breathe through lungs which are evolved from the air-bladder of fishes, which in turn have been evolved from the primitive gullet of the lower forms. There are fishes known which are warm-blooded. Students will kindly remember that the Whale is not a fish, but an aquatic animal—a mammal, in fact, bringing forth its young alive, and suckling it from its breasts.

So we readily see that it is but a step, and a short step at that, between the land-traveling and climbing fishes and the lower forms of Reptiles. The Frog shows us the process of evolution between the two families, its life history reproducing the gradual evolution which may have required ages to perfect in the case of the species. You will remember that the embryo stages of all creatures reproduce the various stages of evolution through which the species has passed—this is true in Man as well as in the Frog.

We need not tarry long in considering the Reptile family of living forms. In its varieties of serpents, lizards, crocodiles, turtles, etc., we have studied and observed its forms. We see the limbless snakes; the lizards with active limbs; the huge, clumsy, slow crocodiles and alligators—the armor-bearing turtles and tortoises—all belonging to the one great family of Reptiles, and nearly all of them being degenerate descendants of the mighty Reptile forms of the geological Age of Reptiles, in which flourished the mighty forms of the giant reptiles—the monsters of land and water. Amidst the dense vegetation of that prehistoric age, surrounded by the most favorable conditions, these mighty creatures flourished and lived, their fossilized skeleton forms evidencing to us how far their descendants have fallen, owing to less favorable conditions, and the development of other life-forms more in harmony with their changed environment.

Next comes the great family of Birds. The Birds ascended from the Reptiles. This is the Eastern Teaching, and this is the teaching of Western Science. It was formerly taught in the text-books that the line of ascent was along the family of winged reptiles which existed in the Age of Reptiles, in the early days of the Earth. But the later writers on the subject, in the Western world, have contradicted this. It is now taught that these ancient winged-reptiles were featherless, and more closely resembled the Bat family than birds. (You will remember that a Bat is neither a reptile nor a bird—it is a mammal, bringing forth its young alive, and suckling them at its breast. The Bat is more like a mouse, and its wings are simply membrane stretched between its fingers, its feet, and its tail.)

The line of ascent from Reptile to Bird was along the forms of the Reptiles that walked on land. There are close anatomical and physiological relations and correspondences between the two families (Reptiles and Birds) which we need not refer to here. And, of course, many modifications have occurred since the "branching-out." The scales of the reptiles, and the feathers of the birds, are known to be but modifications of the original outer skin, as are also the hair, claws, hoofs, nails, etc., of all animals. Even teeth arose in this way, strange as it may now seem—they are all secreted from the skin. What a wonderful field for thought—this gradual evolution from the filmy outer covering of the lowest living forms to the beautiful feathers, beaks, and claws of the bird!

The evolving of wings meant much to the ascending forms of life. The Reptiles were compelled to live in a narrow circle of territory, while the Birds were able to travel over the earth in wide flights. And travel always develops the faculties of observation, memory, etc., and cultivates the senses of seeing, hearing, etc. And the creature is compelled to exercise its evolving "thinking" faculties to a greater extent. And so the Birds were compelled by necessity of their travels to develop a greater degree of thinking organism. The result is that among birds we find many instances of intelligent thought, which cannot be dismissed as "mere instinct." Naturalists place the Crow at the head of the family of Birds, in point of intelligence, and those who have watched these creatures and studied the mental processes, will agree that this is a just decision. It has been proven that Crows are capable of counting up to several figures, and in other ways they display a wonderful degree of almost human sagacity.

Next above the Bird family comes the highest form of all—the Mammals. But before we begin our consideration of these high forms, let us take a hasty glance at the "connecting-links" between the Birds and the Mammals. The lowest forms of the Mammals resemble Birds in many ways. Some of them are toothless, and many of them have the same primitive intestinal arrangements possessed by the birds, from which arises their name, *Monotremes*. These *Monotremes* may be called half-bird and half-mammal. One of the most characteristic of their family is the *Ornithorhynchus,* or Duck-bill, which the early naturalists first thought was a fraud of the taxidermists, or bird-stuffers, and then, when finally convinced, deemed it a "freak-of-nature." But it is not a freak creature, but a "connecting-link" between the two great families of creatures. This animal presents a startling appearance to the observer who witnesses it for the first time. It resembles a beaver, having a soft furry coat, but also has a horny, flat bill like a duck, its feet being webbed, but also furnished with claws projecting over the edge of the web-foot. It lays eggs in an underground nest—two eggs at a time, which are like the eggs of birds, inasmuch as they contain not only the protoplasm from which the embryo is formed, but also the "yolk," on which the embryo feeds until hatched. After the young Duck-bill is hatched, it feeds from teatless glands in the mother's body, the milk being furnished by the mother by a peculiar process. Consider this *miracle—an animal which lays eggs and then when her young are hatched nourishes them with milk.* The milk-glands in the mother are elementary "breasts."

The above-mentioned animal is found in Australia, the land of many strange forms and "connecting-links," which have survived there while in other parts of the globe they have vanished gradually from existence, crowded out by the more perfectly evolved forms. Darwin has called these surviving forms "living fossils." In that same land is also found the *Echdina* or spiny ant-eater, which lays an egg and then hatches it in her pouch, after which she nourishes it on milk, in a manner similar to that of the

Duck-bill. This animal, like the Duck-bill, is a Monotreme.

Scientists are divided in theories as to whether the Monotremes are actually descended directly from the Reptiles or Birds, or whether there was a common ancestor from which Reptiles and Birds and Mammals branched off. But this is not important, for the relationship between Reptiles, Birds and Mammals is clearly proven. And the Monotremes are certainly one of the surviving forms of the intermediate stages.

The next higher step in the ascent of Mammal life above the Monotreme is occupied by the Marsupials, or *milk-giving, pouched animals,* of which family the opossum and kangaroo are well known members. The characteristic feature of this family of creatures is the possession of an external pouch in the female, in which the young are kept and nourished until they can take care of themselves as the young of other animals are able to do. The young of the Marsupials are brought forth, or born, in an imperfect condition, and undeveloped in size and strength. There are fossil remains of Marsupials showing that in past ages creatures of this kind existed which were as large as elephants.

In the more common form of Mammals the young are brought forth fully formed, they having received nourishment, before birth, from the mother's body, through the *placenta,* the appendage which connects the fetus with the parent. The Placental Mammals were the best equipped of all the life-forms for survival and development, for the reason that the young were nourished during their critical period, and the care that the mammal must of necessity give to her young operated in the direction of affording a special protection far superior to that of the other forms. This and other causes acted to place the Placentals in the "Royal line" from which Man was evolved.

The following families of Placental Mammals are recognized by Science, each having its own structural peculiarities:

The *Edentata,* or Toothless creatures, among which are the sloths, ant-eaters, armadillos, etc. These animals seem to be closer to the Monotremes than they are to the Marsupials;

The *Sirenia,* so called by reason of their fanciful resemblance to the sirens of mythology, among which are the sea-cows, manatees, dugongs, etc., which are fish-like in structure and appearance, the fore-limbs being shaped like paddles, or fins, and the hind-limbs being absent or rudimentary;

The *Cetacea,* or Whale Family, including whales, porpoises, dolphins, etc., which are quite fish-like in appearance and structure, their forms being adapted for life in the sea, although they are, of course, Mammals, bringing forth matured young which are suckled at the breast;

The *Ungulata,* or Hoofed Animals, which comprise many varied forms, such as the horse, the tapir, the rhinoceros, the swine, the hippopotamus, the camel, the deer, the sheep, the cow, etc., etc.;

The *Hyracoidea,* which is a small family, the principal member of which is the coney, or rockrabbit, which has teeth resembling those of the hoofed animals, in some ways, and those of the gnawing animals in the others.

The *Proboscidea,* or Trunked Animals, which family is represented in this age only by the families of elephants, which have a peculiar appendage called a "trunk," which they use as an additional limb;

The *Carnivora,* or Flesh-eaters, represented by numerous and various forms, such as the seal, the bear, the weasel, the wolf, the dog, the lion, the tiger, the leopard, etc. The wolf and similar forms belong to the sub-family of dogs; while the lion, tiger, etc., belong to the sub-family of cats;

The *Rodentia,* or Gnawers, comprising the rat, the hare, the beaver, the squirrel, the mouse, etc., etc.;

The *Insectivora,* or Insect Feeders, comprising the mole, the shrew, the hedgehog, etc.;

The *Cheiroptera,* or Finger-Winged Animals, comprising the great family of Bats, etc., which are very highly developed animals;

The *Lemuroidea,* or Lemurs, the name of which is derived from the Latin word meaning a "ghost," by reason of the Lemur's habits of roaming about at night. The Lemur is a nocturnal animal, somewhat resembling the Monkey in general appearance, but with a long, bushy tail and sharp muzzle like a fox. It is akin to a small fox having hands and feet like a monkey, the feet being used to grasp like a hand, as is the case with the true Monkey family. These creatures are classed by some naturalists among the Monkeys by reason of being "four-handed," while others are disposed to consider as still more important their marked relationship with, and affinity to, the marsupials, gnawers and insect-feeders. On the whole, these creatures are strangely organized and come very near to being a "connecting-link" between other forms. One of the Lemurs is what is known as the *colugo,* or "flying lemur," which resembles a squirrel in many particulars, and yet has a membranous web extending from its hands, which enables it to make flying leaps over great distances. This last named variety seems to furnish a link between the insect-feeders and the Primates;

The *Primates,* which is a large family comprising the various forms of monkeys, baboons, man-apes, such as the gibbon, gorilla, chimpanzee, orang-outang, etc., all of which have big jaws, small brains, and a stooping posture. This family also includes MAN, with his big brain and erect posture, and his many races depending upon shape of skull, color of skin, character of hair, etc.

In considering the Ascent of Man (physical) from the lowly forms of the Monera, etc., up to his present high position, the student is struck with the continuity of the ascent, development and unfoldment. While there are many "missing-links," owing to the disappearance of the forms which formed the connection, still there is sufficient proof left in the existing forms to satisfy the fair-minded inquirer. The facts of embryology alone are sufficient proof of the ascent of Man from the lowly forms. Each and every man today has passed through all the forms of the ascent within a few months, from single cell to the new-born, fully formed infant.

Embryology teaches us that the eggs from which all animal forms evolve are all practically alike so far as one can ascertain by microscopic examination, no matter how diverse may be the forms which will evolve from them, and this resemblance is maintained even when the embryo of the higher forms begins to manifest traces of its future form. Von Baer, the German scientist, was the first to note this remarkable and suggestive fact. He stated it in the following words: "In my possession are two little embryos, preserved in alcohol, whose names I have omitted to attach, and at present I am unable to state to what class they belong. They may be lizards, or small birds, or very young mammals, so complete is the similarity in the mode of the formation of the head and trunk in these animals. The extremities, however, are still absent in these embryos. But even if they had existed in the earliest stage of their development, we should learn nothing, for the feet of lizards and mammals, the wings and feet of birds, no less than the hands and feet of man, all arise from the same fundamental form."

As has been said by Prof. Clodd, "the embryos of all living creatures epitomize during development the series of changes through which the ancestral forms passed is their ascent from the simple to the complex; the higher structures passing through the same stages as the lower structures up to the point when they are marked off from them, yet never becoming in detail the form which they represent for the time being. For example, the embryo of man has at the outset gill-like slits on each side of the neck, like a fish. These give place to a membrane like that which supersedes gills in the development of birds and reptiles; the heart is at first a simple pulsating chamber like that in worms; the backbone is prolonged into a movable tail; the great toe is extended, or opposable, like our thumbs, and like the toes of apes; the body three months before birth is covered all over with hair except on the palms and soles. At birth the head is relatively larger, and the arms and legs relatively longer than in the adult; the nose is bridgeless; both features, with others which need not be detailed, being distinctly ape-like. Thus does the egg from which man springs, a structure only one hundred and twenty-fifth of an inch in size, compress into a few weeks the results of millions of years, and set before us the history of his development from fish-like and reptilian forms, and of his more immediate descent from a hairy, tailed quadruped. That which is individual or peculiar to him, the physical and mental character inherited, is left to the slower development which follows birth."

This, then, in brief is the Western theory of Evolution—the Physical Ascent of Man. We have given it as fully as might be in the small space at our disposal in these lessons on the Yogi Philosophy. Why? Because we wish to prove to the Western mind, in the Western way, that Western Science corroborates the Ancient Yogi Teachings of the Unfoldment of Living Forms, from Monad to Man. The Eastern teachers scorn to "prove" anything to their pupils, who sit at the feet of teachers and accept as truth that which is taught them, and which has been handed down from the dim ages long past. But this method will never do for the Western student—he must have it "proven" to him by physical facts and instances, not by keen, subtle, intellectual reasoning alone. The Eastern student wishes to be "told"—the Western student wishes to be "shown." Herein lies the racial differences of method of imparting knowledge. And so we have recognized this fact and have heaped up proof after proof from the pages of Western Science, in order to prove to you the reasonableness, from the Western point of view, of the doctrine of Physical Unfoldment as taught for ages past by the Yogi *gurus* to their *chelas*. You have now the Eastern Teachings on the subject, together with the testimony of Western Science to the reasonableness of the idea.

But, alas! Western Science, while performing a marvelous work in piling up fact after fact to support its newly-discovered theory of Evolution, in a way utterly unknown to the Oriental thinker who seeks after principles by mental concentration—*within* rather than without—while actually proving by physical facts the *mental* conceptions of the Oriental Teachings, still misses the vital point of the subject-thought. In its materialistic tendencies it has failed to recognize *the mental cause of the physical unfoldment.* It is true that Lamark, the real Western discoverer of Evolution, taught that Desire and Mental Craving, was the real force behind Evolution, but his ideas were jeered at by his contemporaries, and are not regarded seriously by the majority of Evolutionists even today. And yet he was nearer to the truth than Darwin or any other Western Evolutionist. And time will show that Science has overlooked his genius, which alone throws the true light upon the subject.

In order to see just this difference between the Darwinian school and the Yogi Teachings let us examine into what causes the Western Evolutionists give for the fact of Evolution itself. We shall do this briefly.

The Darwinians start out to explain the causes of the "Origin of Species," with the statement that "no two individuals of the same species are exactly alike; each tends to vary." This is a self-evident fact, and is very properly used as a starting point for Variation. The next step is then stated as "variations are transmitted, and therefore tend to become permanent," which also is self-evident, and tends to prove the reasonableness of the gradual evolution of species. The next step in the argument is "as man produces new species and forms, by breeding, culture, etc., so has Nature in a longer time produced the same effect, in the same way." This also is reasonable, although it tends to personify Nature, and to give it a *mind* before the evolutionists admit "mind" was evolved.

It will be as well to quote Darwin himself on this point. He says: "As man can produce, and certainly has produced, a great result by his methodical and unconscious means of selection, what may not natural selection effect? Man can act only on external and visible characters, while Nature, if I may be allowed to personify the natural preservation or survival of the fittest, cares nothing for appearances except in so far as they are useful to any being. She can act on every internal organ, on every shade of constitutional difference, on the whole machinery of life. Man selects only for his own good; Nature only for the good of the being which she tends. Every selected character is fully exercised by her, as is implied by the fact of their selection. Man keeps the natives of many climates in the same country; he seldom exercises each selected character in some peculiar and fitting manner; he feeds a long-beaked and a short-beaked pigeon on the same food; he does not exercise a long-backed or long-legged quadruped in any peculiar manner; he exposes sheep with long hair and short wool in the same climate. He does not allow the most vigorous males to struggle for the females. He does not rigidly destroy all inferior animals, but protects during each varying season, so far as lies in his power, all his productions. He often begins his selection by some half-monstrous form, or at least by some modification prominent enough to catch the eye or to be plainly useful to him. Under Nature the slightest differences of structure or constitution may well turn the nicely balanced scale in the struggle for life, and so be preserved. How fleeting are the wishes and efforts of man! how short his time! and consequently how poor will be his results, compared with those accumulated by nature during whole geological periods! Can we wonder, then, that Nature's productions should be far 'truer' in character than man's productions; that they should be infinitely better adapted to the most complex conditions of life, and should plainly bear the stamp of far higher workmanship?"

Darwin's theory of survival of the fittest is begun by the statement of the fact that the number of organisms that survive are very small compared with the number that are born. To quote his own words, "There is no exception to the rule that every organic being naturally increases at so high a rate that, if not destroyed, the earth would soon be covered by the progeny of a single pair. Even slow-breeding man has doubled in twenty-five years, and at this rate in less than a thousand years there would literally not be standing room for the progeny." It has been computed that if the offspring of the elephant, which is believed to be the slowest breeding animal known, were to survive, there would be about 20,000,000 elephants on the earth in 750 years. The roe of a single cod contains eight or nine millions of eggs, and if each egg were to hatch, and the fish survive, the sea would shortly become a solid mass of codfish. The house fly is said to have 20,000,000 descendants in a season, counting several generations of progeny, from its several broods. And some scientist has computed that the *aphis*, or plant-louse, breeds so rapidly, and in such enormous quantity, that the tenth generation of one set of parents would be so large that it would contain more ponderable animal matter than would the population of China, which is estimated at 500,000,000! And this without counting the progeny preceding the tenth generation!

The result of the above conditions is very plain. There must ensue a Struggle for Existence, which necessitates the Survival of the Fittest. The weak are crushed out by the strong; the swift out-distance the slow. The individual forms or species best adapted to their environment and best equipped for the struggle, be the equipment physical or mental, survive those less well equipped or less well adapted to environment. Animals evolving variations in structure that give them even a slight advantage over others not so favored, naturally have a better chance to survive. And this, briefly, is what Evolutionists call "The Survival of the Fittest."

As appertaining to the Struggle for Existence, color and mimicry are important factors. Grant Allen, in his work on Darwin, says concerning this, and also as illustrating "Natural Selection": "In the desert with its monotonous sandy coloring, a black insect or a white insect, still more a red insect or a blue insect, would be immediately detected and devoured by its natural enemies, the birds and the lizards. But any greyish or yellowish insects would be less likely to attract attention at first sight, and would be overlooked as long as there were any more conspicuous individuals of their own kind about for the birds and lizards to feed on. Hence, in a very short time the desert would be depopulated of all but the greyest and yellowest insects; and among these the birds would pick out those which differed most markedly in hue and shade from the sand around them. But those which happened to vary most in the direction of a sandy or spotty color would be more likely to survive, and to become the parents of future generations. Thus, in the course of long ages, all the insects which inhabit deserts have become sand-colored, because the less sandy were perpetually picked out for destruction by their ever-watchful foes, while the most sandy escaped, and multiplied and replenished the earth with their own likes."

Prof. Clodd, remarking upon this fact, adds: "Thus, then, is explained the tawny color of the larger animals that inhabit the desert; the stripes upon the tiger, which parallel with the vertical stems of bamboo, conceal him as he stealthily nears his prey; the brilliant green of tropical birds; the leaf-like form and colors of certain insects; the dried, twig-like form of many caterpillars; the bark-like appearance of tree-frogs; the harmony of the ptarmigan's summer plumage with the lichen-colored stones upon which it sits; the dusky color of creatures that haunt the night; the bluish transparency of animals which live on the surface of the sea; the gravel-like color of flat-fish that live at the bottom; and the gorgeous tints of those that swim among the coral reefs."

All this does not run contrary to the Yogi Philosophy, although the latter would regard these things as but the secondary cause for the variation and survival of species, etc. The Oriental teachings are that it is the *desire* of the animal that *causes* it to assume the colors and shapes in accordance with its environment, the desire of course operating along sub-conscious lines of physical manifestation. The mental influence, which is the real cause of the phenomena, and which is taught as such by the Yogis, is almost lost sight of by the Western Evolutionists, who are apt to regard Mind as a "by-product" of matter. On the contrary, *the Yogis regard Matter as the product of Mind.* But there is no conflict here as far as regards the law of the Survival of the Fittest. The insects that *most desired* to become sand-colored became so, and were thus protected, while their less "desireful" brethren were exterminated. The Western scientist explains the outward phenomena, but does not look for the *cause* behind it, which is taught by the Oriental sages.

The doctrine of "Sexual Selection" is another of the leading tenets of the Darwinists. Briefly, it may be expressed as the theory that in the rivalry and struggle of the males for the females the strongest males win the day, and thus transmit their particular qualities to their offspring. Along the same lines is that of the attraction exerted by bright colors in the plumage of the males of birds, etc., which give them an advantage in the eyes of the females, and thus, naturally, the bright colors are perpetuated.

This, then, is the brief outline of the Story of Man's Physical Evolution, as stated by Western Science, and compared with the Yogi Teachings. The student should compare the two ideas, that he may harmonize and reconcile them. It must be remembered, however, that Darwin did *not* teach that Man descended from the monkeys, or apes, as we know them now. The teaching of Western Evolution is that the apes, and higher forms of monkey life descended from some common ancestral form, which same ancestor was also the ancestor of Man. In other words, Man and Apes are the different branches that emerged from the common trunk ages ago. Other forms doubtless emerged from the same trunk, and perished because less adapted to their environments. The Apes were best adapted to their own environments, and Man was best adapted to his. The weaker branches failed.

One must remember that the most savage races known to us today are practically as far different from the highest American, European or Hindu types of Man as from the highest Apes. Indeed, it would seem far easier for a high Ape to evolve into a Kaffir,

Hottentot, or Digger Indian, than for the latter to evolve into an Emerson, Shakespeare, or Hindu Sage. As Huxley has shown, the brain-structure of Man compared with that of the Chimpanzee shows differences but slight when compared with the difference between that of the Chimpanzee and that of the Lemur. The same authority informs us that in the important feature of the deeper brain furrows, and intricate convolutions, the chasm between the highest civilized man and the lowest savage is far greater than between the lowest savage and the highest man-like ape. Darwin, describing the Fuegians, who are among the very lowest forms of savages, says: "Their very signs and expressions are less intelligible to us than those of the domesticated animal. They are men who do not possess the instinct of those animals, nor yet appear to boast of human reason, or at least of arts consequent upon that reason."

Professor Clodd, in describing the "primitive man," says: "Doubtless he was lower than the lowest of the savages of today—a powerful, cunning biped, with keen sense organs always sharper, in virtue of constant exercise, in the savage than in the civilized man (who supplements them by science), strong instincts, uncontrolled and fitful emotions, small faculty of wonder, and nascent reasoning power; unable to forecast tomorrow, or to comprehend yesterday, living from hand to mouth on the wild products of Nature, clothed in skin and bark, or daubed with clay, and finding shelter in trees and caves; ignorant of the simpiest arts, save to chip a stone missle, and perhaps to produce fire; strong in his needs of life and vague sense of right to it and to what he could get, but slowly impelled by common perils and passions to form ties, loose and haphazard at the outset, with his kind, the power of combination with them depending on sounds, signs and gestures."

Such was the ancestral man. Those who are interested in him are referred to the two wonderful tales of the cave-man written in the form of stories by two great modern novelists. The books referred to are (1) *"The Story of Ab,"* by Stanley Waterloo, and (2) *"Before Adam,"* by Jack London. They may be obtained from any bookseller. Both are works of fiction, with the scientific facts cleverly interwoven into them.

And now in conclusion before we pass on the subject of "Spiritual Evolution," which will form the subject of our next lesson, we would again call your attention to the vital difference between the Western and the Eastern Teachings. The Western holds to a mechanical theory of life, which works without the necessity of antecedent Mind, the latter appearing as a "product" at a certain stage. The Eastern holds *that Mind is back of, under, and antecedent to all the work of Evolution*—the *cause*, not the effect or product. The Western claims that Mind was produced by the struggle of Matter to produce higher forms of itself. *The Eastern claims that the whole process of Evolu-*

tion is caused by Mind striving, struggling and pressing forward toward expressing itself more fully—to liberate itself from the confining and retarding Matter—the struggle resulting in an Unfoldment which causes sheath after sheath of the confining material bonds to be thrown off and discarded, in the effort to release the confined Spirit which is behind even the Mind. The Yogi Teachings are that the Evolutionary Urge is the pressure of the confined Spirit striving to free itself from the fetters and bonds which sorely oppress it.

The struggle and pain of Evolution is the parturition-pangs of the Spiritual deliverance from the womb of Matter. Like all birth it is attended by pain and suffering, but the end justifies it all. And as the human mother forgets her past suffering in the joy of witnessing the face, and form, and life, of her loved child, so will the soul forget the pain of the Spiritual birth by reason of the beauty and nobility of that which will be born to and from it.

Let us study well the story of Physical Evolution, but let us not lose ourselves in it, for it is but the preliminary to the story of the Unfoldment of the Soul.

Let us not despise the tale of the Body of Man—for it is the story of the Temple of the Spirit which has been built up from the most humble beginnings, until it has reached the present high stage. And yet even this is but the beginning, for the work will go on, and on, and on, in the spirit of those beautiful lines of Holmes:

"Build thee more stately mansions, oh, my soul!
As the swift seasons roll!
Leave thy low-vaulted past!
Let each new temple, nobler than the last,
Shut thee from heaven with a dome more vast,
Till thou at last *art free*,
Leaving thine outgrown shell by life's unresting sea."

THE NINTH LESSON

METEMPSYCHOSIS.

As we have said in our last lesson, while the Yogi Teachings throw an important light upon the Western theory of Evolution, still there is a vital difference between the Western scientific teachings on the subject and the Eastern theories and teachings. The Western idea is that the process is a mechanical, material one, and that "mind" is a "by-product" of Matter in its evolution. But the Eastern Teachings hold that Mind is under, back of, and antecedent to all the work of Evolution, and that Matter is a "by-product" of Mind, rather than the reverse.

The Eastern Teachings hold that Evolution is caused by Mind striving, struggling, and pressing forward toward fuller and fuller expression, using Matter as a material, and yet always struggling to free itself from the confining and retarding influence of the latter. The struggle results in an Unfoldment, causing sheath after sheath of the confining material bonds to be thrown off and discarded, as the Spirit presses upon the Mind, and the Mind moulds and shapes the Matter. Evolution is but the process of birth of the Individualized Spirit, from the web of Matter in which it has been confined. And the pains and struggles are but incidents of the spiritual parturition.

In this and following lessons we shall consider the "Spiritual Evolution, of the race—that is the Unfoldment of Individualized Spirit—just as we did the subject Physical Evolution in the last two lessons.

We have seen that preceding Spiritual Evolution, there was a Spiritual Involution. The Yogi Philosophy holds that in the Beginning, the Absolute meditated upon the subject of Creation, and formed a Mental Image, or Thought-Form, of an Universal Mind—that is, of an Universal Principle of Mind. This Universal Principle of Mind is the Great Ocean of "Mind-Stuff" from which all the phenomenal Universe is evolved. From this Universal Principle of Mind, proceeded the Universal Principle of Force or Energy. And from the latter, proceeded the Universal Principle of Matter.

The Universal Principle of Mind was bound by Laws imposed upon it by the mental-conception of the Absolute—the Cosmic Laws of Nature. And these laws were the compelling causes of the Great Involution. For before Evolution was possible, Involution was necessary. We have explained that the word "involve" means "to wrap up; to cover; to hide, etc." Before a thing can be "evolved," that is "unfolded," it must first be "involved," that is "wrapped up." A thing must be *put in,* before it may be *taken out.*

Following the laws of Involution imposed upon it, the Universal Mental Principle involved itself in the Universal Energy Principle; and then in obedience to the same laws, the latter involved itself in the Universal Material Principle. Each stage of Involution, or *wrapping-up,* created for itself (out of the higher principle which in being involved) the wrapper or sheath which is to be used to wrap-up the higher principle. And the higher forms of the Material Principle formed sheaths of lower forms, until forms of Matter were produced far more gross than any known to us now, for they have disappeared in the Evolutionary ascent. Down, down, down went the process of Involution, until the lowest point was reached. Then ensued a moment's pause, preceding the beginning of the Evolutionary Unfoldment.

Then began the Great Evolution. But, as we have told you, the Upward movement was distinguished by the "Tendency toward Individualization." That is, while the Involuntary Process was accomplished by Principles as Principles, the Upward Movement was begun by a tendency toward "splitting up," and the creation of "individual forms," and the effort to perfect them and build upon them higher and still higher succeeding forms, until a stage was reached in which the Temple of the Spirit was worthy of being occupied by Man, the self-conscious expression of the Spirit. For the coming of Man was the first step of a higher form of Evolution—the Spiritual Evolution. Up to this time there had been simply an Evolution of Bodies, but now there came the Evolution of Souls.

And this Evolution of Souls becomes possible only by the process of Metempsychosis (pronounced *me-temp-si-ko-sis*) which is more commonly known as Reincarnation, or Reembodiment.

It becomes necessary at this point to call your attention to the general subject of Metempsychosis, for the reason that the public mind is most confused regarding this important subject. It has the most vague ideas regarding the true teachings, and has somehow acquired the impression that the teachings are that human souls are re-born into the bodies of dogs, and other animals. The wildest ideas on this subject are held by some people. And, not only is this so, but even a number of those who hold to the doctrine of Reincarnation, in some of its forms, hold that their individual souls were once the individual souls of animals, from which state they have evolved to the present condition. This last is a perversion of the highest Yogi Teachings, and we trust to make same plain in these lessons. But, first we must take a look at the general subject of Metempsychosis, that we may see the important part it has played in the field of human thought and belief.

While to many the idea of Metempsychosis may seem new and unfamiliar, still it is one of the oldest conceptions of the race, and in ages past was the accepted belief of the whole of the civilized race of man of the period. And even today, it is accepted as Truth by the majority of the race

The almost universal acceptance of the idea by the East with its teeming life, counterbalances its comparative non-reception by the Western people of the day. From the early days of written or legendery history, Metempsychosis has been the accepted belief of many of the most intelligent of the race. It is found underlying the magnificent civilization of ancient Egypt, and from thence it traveled to the Western world being held as the highest truth by such teachers as Pythagoras, Empedocles, Plato, Virgil and Ovid. Plato's Dialogues are full of this teaching. The Hindus have always held to it. The Persians, inspired by their learned Magi, accepted it implicitly. The ancient Druids, and Priests of Gaul, as well as the ancient inhabitants of Germany, held to it. Traces of it may be found in the remains of the Aztec, Peruvian and Mexican civilizations.

The Eleusinian Mysteries of Greece, the Roman Mysteries, and the Inner Doctrines of the Cabbala of the Hebrews all taught the Truths of Metempsychosis. The early Christian Fathers; the Gnostic and Manichaeans and other sects of the Early Christian people, all held to the doctrine. The modern German philosophers have treated it with the greatest respect, if indeed they did not at least partially accept it. Many modern writers have considered it gravely, and with respect. The following quotations will give an idea of "how the wind is blowing" in the West:

"Of all the theories respecting the origin of the soul, Metempsychosis seems to me the most plausible and therefore the one most likely to throw light on the question of a life to come."—*Frederick H. Hedge.*

"It would be curious if we should find science and philosophy taking up again the old theory of metempsychosis, remodelling it to suit our present modes of religious and scientific thought, and launching it again on the wide ocean of human belief. But stranger things have happened in the history of human opinions."—*James Freeman Clarke.*

"If we could legitimately determine any question of belief by the number of its adherents, the * * * * would apply to metempsychosis more fitly than to any other. I think it is quite as likely to be revived and to come to the front as any rival theory."—*Prof. Wm. Knight.*

"It seems to me, a firm and well-grounded faith in the doctrine of Christian metempsychosis might help to regenerate the world. For it would be a faith not hedged around with many of the difficulties and objections which beset other forms of doctrine, and it offers distinct and pungent motives for trying to lead a more Christian life, and for loving and helping our brother-man."—*Prof. Francis Bowen.*

"The doctrine of Metempsychosis may almost claim to be a natural or innate belief in the human mind, if we may judge from its wide diffusion among the nations of the earth, and its prevalence throughout the historical ages."—*Prof. Francis Bowen.*

"When Christianity first swept over Europe, the inner thought of its leaders was deeply tinctured with this truth. The Church tried ineffectually to eradicate it, but in various sects it kept sprouting forth beyond the time of Erigina and Bonaventura, its mediaeval advocates. Every great intuitional soul, as Paracelsus, Boehme, and Swedenborg, has adhered to it. The Italian luminaries, Giordano Bruno and Campanella, embraced it. The best of German philosophy is enriched by it. In Schopenhauer, Lessing, Hegel, Leibnitz, Herder, and Fichte, the younger, it is earnestly advocated. The anthropological systems of Kant and Schelling furnish points of contact with it. The younger Helmont, in *De Revolutione Animarum,* adduces in two hundred problems all the arguments which may be urged in favor of the return of souls into human bodies according to Jewish ideas. Of English thinkers, the Cambridge Platonists defended it with much learning and acuteness, most conspicuously Henry More; and in Cudworth and Hume it ranks as the most rational theory of immortality. Glanvil's *Lux Orientalis* devotes a curious treatise to it. It captivated the minds of Fourier and Leroux. Andre Pezzani's book on *The Plurality of the Soul's Lives* works out the system on the Roman Catholic idea of expiation."—E. D. WALKER, in *"Re-Incarnation, a Study of Forgotten Truth."*

And in the latter part of the Nineteenth Century, and this the early part of the Twentieth Century, the general public has been made familiar with the idea of Metempsychosis, under the name of Re-incarnation, by means of the great volume of literature issued by The Theosophical Society and its allied following. No longer is the thought a novelty to the Western thinker, and many have found within themselves a corroborative sense of its truth. In fact, to many the mere mention of the idea has been sufficient to awaken faint shadowy memories of past lives, and, to such, many heretofore unaccountable traits of character, tastes, inclinations, sympathies, dislikes, etc., have been explained.

The Western world has been made familiar with the idea of the re-birth of souls into new bodies, under the term of "Re-incarnation," which means "a re-entry into flesh," the word "incarnate" being derived from the words *"in,"* and *"carnis,"* meaning flesh—the English word meaning "to clothe with flesh," etc. The word Metempsychosis, which we use in this lesson, is concerned rather with the "passage of the soul" from one tenement to another, the "fleshly" idea being merely incidental.

The doctrine of Metempsychosis, or Re-incarnation, together with its accompanying doctrine, Karma, or Spiritual Cause and Effect, is one of the great foundation stones of the Yogi Philosophy, as indeed it is of the entire system of systems of Oriental Philosophy and Thought. Unless one understands Metempsychosis he will never be able to understand the Eastern Teachings, for he will be without the Key. You who have read the *Bhagavad Gita,* that wonderful Hindu Epic, will remember how the thread of Re-Birth runs through it all. You remember the words of *Krishna* to *Arjuna*: "As the soul, wearing this material body, experienceth the stages of infancy, youth, manhood, and old age, even so shall it, in due time, pass on to another body, and in other incarnations shall it again live, and move and play its part." "These bodies, which act as enveloping coverings for the souls occupying them, are but finite things—things of the moment—and not the Real Man at all. They perish as all finite things perish—let them perish." "As a man throweth away his old garments, replacing them with new and brighter ones, even so the Dweller of the body, having quitted its old mortal frame, entereth into others which are new and freshly prepared for it. Weapons pierce not the Real Man, nor doth the fire burn him; the water affecteth him not, nor the wind drieth him nor bloweth him away. For he is impregnable and impervious to these things of the world of change—he is eternal, permanent, unchangeable, and unalterable—Real."

This view of life gives to the one who holds to it, an entirely different mental attitude. He no longer identifies himself with the particular body that he may be occupying, nor with any other body for that matter. He learns to regard his body just as he would a garment which he is wearing, useful to him for certain purposes, but which will in time be discarded and thrown aside for a better one, and one better adapted to his new requirements and needs. So firmly is this idea embedded in the consciousness of the Hindus, that they will often say "My body is tired," or "My body is hungry," or "My body is full of energy," rather than that "I am" this or that thing. And this consciousness, once attained, gives to one a sense of strength, security and power unknown to him who regards his body as himself. The first step for the student who wishes to grasp the idea of Metempsychosis, and who wishes to awaken in his consciousness a certainty of its truth, is to familiarize himself with the idea of his "I" being a thing independent and a part from his body, although using the latter as an abiding place and a useful shelter and instrument for the time being.

Many writers on the subject of Metempsychosis have devoted much time, labor and argument to prove the reasonableness of the doctrine upon purely speculative, philosophical, or metaphysical grounds. And while we believe that such efforts are praiseworthy for the reason that many persons must be first convinced in that way, still we feel that one must really *feel* the truth of the doctrine from something within his own consciousness, before he will really *believe* it to be truth. One may convince himself of the logical necessity of the doctrine of Metempsychosis, but at the same time he may drop the matter with a shrug of the shoulders and a "still, who knows?" But when one begins to feel within himself the awakening consciousness of a "something in the past," not to speak of the flashes of memory, and feeling of former acquaintance with the subject, then, and then only, does he begin to *believe.*

Many people have had "peculiar experiences" that are accountable only upon the hypothesis of Metempyschosis. Who has not experienced the consciousness of having *felt the thing before—having thought it some time in the dim past? Who has not witnessed new scenes that appear old, very old? Who has not met persons for the first time, whose presence awak-*

ened memories of a past lying far back in the misty ages of long ago? Who has not been seized at times with the consciousness of a mighty "oldness" of soul? Who has not heard music, often entirely new compositions, which somehow awakens memories of similar strains, scenes, places, faces, voices, lands, associations and events, sounding dimly on the strings of memory as the breezes of the harmony floats over them? Who has not gazed at some old painting, or piece of statuary, with the sense of having seen it all before? Who has not lived through events, which brought with them a certainty of being merely a repetition of some shadowy occurrences away back in lives lived long ago? Who has not felt the influence of the mountain, the sea, the desert, coming to them when they are far from such scenes—coming so vividly as to cause the actual scene of the present to fade into comparative unreality. Who has not had these experiences—who we ask?

Writers, poets, and others who carry messages to the world, have testified to these things—and nearly every man or woman who hears the message recognizes it as something having correspondence in his or her own life. Sir Walter Scott tells us in his diary: "I cannot, I am sure, tell if it is worth marking down, that yesterday, at dinner time, I was strangely haunted by what I would call the sense of preexistence, viz., a confused idea that nothing that passed was said for the first time; that the same topics had been discussed and the same persons had stated the same opinions on them. The sensation was so strong as to resemble what is called the mirage in the desert and a calenture on board ship." The same writer, in one of his novels, "Guy Mannering," makes one of his characters say: "Why is it that some scenes awaken thoughts which belong as it were, to dreams of early and shadowy recollections, such as old Brahmin moonshine would have ascribed to a state of previous existence. How often do we find ourselves in society which we have never before met, and yet feel impressed with a mysterious and ill-defined consciousness that neither the scene nor the speakers nor the subject are entirely new; nay, feel as if we could anticipate that part of the conversation which has not yet taken place."

Bulwer speaks of "that strange kind of inner and spiritual memory which so often recalls to us places and persons we have never seen before, and which Platonists would resolve to be the unquenched consciousness of a former life." And again, he says: "How strange is it that at times a feeling comes over us as we gaze upon certain places, which associates the scene either with some dim remembered and dreamlike images of the Past, or with a prophetic and fearful omen of the Future. Every one has known a similar strange and indistinct feeling at certain times and places, and with a similar inability to trace the cause." Poe has written these words on the subject: "We walk about, amid the destinies of our world existence, accompanied by dim but ever present memories of a Destiny more vast—very distant in the bygone time and infinitely awful. We live out a youth peculiarly haunted by such dreams, yet never mistaking them for dreams. As memories we know them. During our youth the distinctness is too clear to deceive us even for a moment. But the doubt of manhood dispels these feelings as illusions."

Home relates an interesting incident in his life, which had a marked effect upon his beliefs, thereafter. He relates that upon an occasion when he visited a strange house in London he was shown into a room to wait. He says: "On looking around, to my astonishment everything appeared perfectly familiar to me. I seemed to recognize every object. I said to myself, 'What is this? I have never been here before, and yet I have seen all this, and if so, then there must be a very peculiar knot in that shutter.'" He proceeded to examine the shutter, and much to his amazement the knot was there.

We have recently heard of a similar case, told by an old lady who formerly lived in the far West of the United States. She states that upon one occasion a party was wandering on the desert in her part of the country, and found themselves out of water. As that part of the desert was unfamiliar even to the guides, the prospect for water looked very poor indeed. After a fruitless search of several hours, one of the party, a perfect stranger to that part of the country, suddenly pressed his hand to his head, and acted in a dazed manner, crying out "I know that a water-hole is over to the right—this way," and away he started with the party after him. After a half-hour's journey they reached an old hidden water-hole that was unknown even to the oldest man in the party. The stranger said that he did not understand the matter, but that he had somehow experienced a sensation of *having been there before,* and knowing just where the water-hole was located. An old Indian who was questioned about the matter, afterward, stated that the place had been well known to his people who formerly travelled much on that part of the desert; and that they had legends relating to the "hidden water-hole," running back for many generations. In this case, it was remarked that the water-hole was situated in such a peculiar and unusual manner, as to render it almost undiscoverable even to people familiar with the characteristics of that part of the country. The old lady who related the story, had it direct from the lips of one of the party, who regarded it as "something queer," but who had never even heard of Metempsychosis.

A correspondent of an English magazine writes as follows: "A gentleman of high intellectual attainments, now deceased, once told me that he had dreamed of being in a strange city, so vividly that he remembered the streets, houses and public buildings as distinctly as those of any place he ever visited. A few weeks later he was induced to visit a panorama in Leicester Square, when he was startled by seeing the city of which he had dreamed. The likeness was perfect, except that one additional church appeared in the picture. He was so struck by the circumstance that he spoke to the exhibitor, assuming for the purpose the air of a traveller acquainted with the place, when he was informed that the church was a recent erection." The fact of the addition of the church, seems to place the incident within the rule of awakened memories of scenes known in a past life, for clairvoyance, astral travel, etc., would show the scene as it was at the time of the dream, not as it had been years before.

Charles Dickens mentions a remarkable impression in his work "Pictures from Italy." "In the foreground was a group of silent peasant girls, leaning over the parapet of the little bridge, looking now up at the sky, now down into the water; in the distance a deep dell; the shadow of an approaching night on everything. If I had been murdered there in some former life I could not have seemed to remember the place more thoroughly, or with more emphatic chilling of the blood; and the real remembrance of it acquired in that minute is so strengthened by the imaginary recollection that I hardly think I could forget it."

We have recently met two people in America who had very vivid memories of incidents in their past life. One of these, a lady, has a perfect horror of large bodies of water, such as the Great Lakes, or the Ocean, although she was born and has lived the greater part of her life inland, far removed from any great body of water. She has a distinct recollection of falling from a large canoe-shape vessel, of peculiar lines, and drowning. She was quite overcome upon her first visit to the Field Museum in Chicago, where there were exhibited a number of models of queer vessels used by primitive people. She pointed out one similar in shape, and lines, to the one she remembers as having fallen from in some past life.

The second case mentioned is that of a married couple who met each other in a country foreign to both, on their travels. They fell in love with each other, and both have felt that their marriage was a reunion rather than a new attachment. The husband one day shortly after their marriage told his wife in a rather shamed-faced way that he had occasional flashes of memory of having held in his arms, in the dim past, a woman whose face he could not recall, but who wore a strange necklace, he describing the details of the latter. The wife said nothing, but after her husband had left for his office, she went to the attic and unpacked an old trunk containing some odds and ends, relics, heirlooms, etc., and drew from it an old necklace of peculiar pattern that her grandfather had brought back from India, where he had lived in his younger days, and which had been in the family ever since. She laid the necklace on the table, so that her husband would see it upon his return. The moment his eyes fell upon it, he turned white as death, and gasped "My God! *that's the necklace!*"

A writer in a Western journal gives the following story of a Southern woman. "When I was in Heidelberg, Germany, attending a convention of Mystics, in company with some friends I paid my first visit to the ruined Heidelberg Castle. As I approached it I was impressed with the existence of a peculiar room in an inaccessible portion of the building. A paper and pencil were provided me, and I drew a diagram of the room even to its peculiar floor. My diagram and description were perfect, when we afterwards visited the room. In some way, not yet clear to me, I have been connected with that apartment. Still another impression came to me with regard to a book, which I was made to feel was in the old library of the Heidelberg University. I not only knew what the book was, but even felt that a certain name of an old German professor would be found written in it. Communicating this feeling to one of the Mystics at the convention, a search was made for the volume, but it was not found. Still the impression clung to me, and another effort was made to find the book; this time we were rewarded for our pains. Sure enough, there on the margin of one of the leaves was the very name I had been given in such a strange manner. Other things at the same time went to convince me that I was in possession of the soul of a person who had known Heidelberg two or three centuries ago."

A contributor to an old magazine relates, among other instances, the following regarding a friend who remembers having died in India during the youth of some former life. He states: "He sees the bronzed attendants gathered about his cradle in their white dresses; they are fanning him. And as they gaze he passes into unconsciousness. Much of his description concerned points of which he knew nothing from any other source, but all was true to the life, and enabled me to fix on India as the scene which he recalled."

While comparatively few among the Western races are able to remember more than fragments of their past lives, in India it is quite common for a man well developed spiritually to clearly remember the incidents and details of former incarnations, and the evidence of the awakening ot such power causes little more than passing interest among his people. There is, as we shall see later, a movement toward conscious Metempsychosis, and many of the race are just moving on to that plane. In India the highly developed individuals grow into a clear recollection of their past lives when they reach the age of puberty, and when their brains are developed sufficiently to grasp the knowledge locked up in the depths of the soul. In the meantime the individual's memory of the past is locked away in the recesses of his mind, just as are many facts and incidents of his present life so locked away, to be remembered only when some one mentions the subject, or some circumstance serves to supply the associative link to the apparently forgotten matter.

Regarding the faculty of memory in our present lives, we would quote the following from the pen of Prof. William Knight, printed in the Fortnightly Review. He says: "Memory of the details of the past is absolutely impossible. The power of the conservative faculty, though relatively great, is extremely limited. We forget the larger portion of experience soon after we have passed through it, and we should be able to recall the particulars of our past years, filling all the missing links of consciousness since we entered on the present life, before we were in a position to remember our ante-natal experience. Birth must necessarily be preceded by crossing the river of oblivion, while the capacity for fresh acquisition survives, and the garnered wealth of old experience determines the amount and character of the new."

Another startling evidence of the proof of Metempsychosis is afforded us in the cases of "infant prodigies," etc., which defy any other explanation. Take the cases of the manifestation of musical talent in certain children at an early age, for instance. Take the case of Mozart who at the age of four was able to not only perform difficult pieces on the piano, but actually composed original works of merit. Not only did he manifest the highest faculty of sound and note, but also an instinctive ability to compose and arrange music, which ability was superior to that of many men who had devoted years of their life to study and practice. The laws of harmony—the science of commingling tones, was to him not the work of years, but a faculty born in him. There are many similar cases of record.

Heredity does not explain these instances of genius, for in many of the recorded cases, none of the ancestors manifested any talent or ability. From whom did Shakespeare inherit his genius? From whom did Plato derive his wonderful thought? From what ancestor did Abraham Lincoln inherit his character—coming from a line of plain, poor, hard-working people, and possessing all of the physical attributes and characteristics of his ancestry, he, nevertheless, manifested a mind which placed him among the foremost of his race. Does not Metempsychosis give us the only possible key? Is it not reasonable to suppose that the abilities displayed by the infant genius, and the talent of the men who spring from obscure origin, have their root in the experiences of a previous life?

Then take the cases of children at school. Children of even the same family manifest different degrees of receptivity to certain studies. Some "take to" one thing, and some to another. Some find arithmetic so easy that they almost absorb it intuitively, while grammar is a hard task for them; while their brothers and sisters find the exact reverse to be true. How many have found that when they would take up some new study, it is almost like recalling something already learned. Do you student, who are now reading these lines take your own case. Does not all this Teaching seem to you like the repetition of some lesson learned long ago? Is it not like remembering something already learned, rather than the learning of some new truth? Were you not attracted to these studies. in the first place, by a feeling that you had known it all before, somewhere, somehow? Does not your mind leap ahead of the lesson, and see what is coming next, long before you have turned the pages? These inward evidences of the fact of pre-existence are so strong that they outweigh the most skillful appeal to the intellect.

This intuitive knowledge of the truth of Metempsychosis explains why the belief in it is sweeping over the Western world at such a rapid rate. The mere mention of the idea, to many people who have never before heard of it, is sufficient to cause them to recognize its truth. And though they may not understand the laws of its operation, yet deep down in their consciousness they find a something that convinces them of its truth. In spite of the objections that are urged against the teaching, it is making steady headway and progress.

The progress of the belief in Metempsychosis however has been greatly retarded by the many theories and dogmas attached to it by some of the teachers. Not to speak of the degrading ideas of re-birth into the bodies of animals, etc., which have polluted the spring of Truth, there are to be found many other features of teaching and theory which repel people, and cause them to try to kill out of the minds the glimmer of Truth that they find there. The human soul instinctively revolts against the teaching that it is bound to the wheel or re-birth, *willy-nilly*, compulsorily, without choice—compelled to live in body after body until great cycles are past. The soul, perhaps already sick of earth-life, and longing to pass on to higher planes of existence, fights against such teaching. And it does well to so fight, for the truth is nearer to its hearts desire. There is no soul longing that does not carry with it the prophecy of its own fulfillment, and so it is in this case. It is true that the soul of one filled with earthly desires, and craving for material things, will by the very force of those desires be drawn back to earthly re-birth in a body best suited for the gratification of the longings, desires and cravings that it finds within itself. But it is likewise true that the earth-sick soul is not compelled to return unless its own desires bring it back. Desire is the key note of Metempsychosis, although up to a certain stage it may operate unconsciously. The sum of the desires of a soul regulate its re-birth. Those who have become sickened of all that earth has for them at this stage of its evolution, may, and do, rest in states of existence far removed from earth scenes, until the race progresses far enough to afford the resting soul the opportunities and environments that it so earnestly craves.

And more than this, when Man reaches a certain stage, the process of Metempsychosis no longer remains unconscious, but he enters into a conscious knowing, willing passage from one life to another. And when that stage is reached a full memory of the past lives is unfolded, and life to such a soul becomes as the life of a day, succeeded by a night, and then the awakening into another day with full knowledge and recollection of the events of the day before. We are in merely the babyhood of the race now, and the fuller life of the conscious soul lies before us. Yea, even now it is being entered into by the few of the race that have progressed sufficiently far on the Path. And you, student, who feel within you that craving for conscious re-birth and future spiritual evolution, and the distaste for, and horror of, a further blind, unconscious re-plunge into the earth-life—know you, that this longing on your part is but an indication of what lies before you. It is the strange, subtle, awakening of the nature within you, which betokens the higher state. Just as the young person feels within his or her body strange emotions, longings and stirrings, which betoken the passage from the child state into that of manhood or womanhood, so do these spiritual longings, desires and cravings betoken the passage from unconscious re-birth into conscious knowing Metempsychosis, when you have passed from the scene of your present labors.

In our next lesson we shall consider the history of the race as its souls passed on from the savage tribes to the man of to-day. It is the history of the race—the history of the individual—your own history, student—the record of that through which you have passed to become that which you now are. And as you have climbed step after step up the arduous path, so will you, hereafter climb still higher paths, but no longer in unconsciousness, but with your spiritual eyes wide open to the Rays of Truth pouring forth from the great Central Sun—the Absolute.

Concluding this lesson, we would quote two selections from the American poet, Whitman, whose strange genius was undoubtedly the result of vague memories springing from a previous life, and which burst into utterances often not more than half understood by the mind that gave them birth. Whitman says:

"Facing West from California's shores,
Inquiring, tireless, seeking what is yet unfound,
A, a child, very old, over waves, toward the house of maternity, the land of migrations, look afar,
Look off the shores of my Western sea, the circle almost circled:
For starting Westward from Hindustan, from the vales of Kashmere,
From Asia, from the north, from God, the sage, and the hero,
From the south, from the flowery peninsulas and spice islands,
Long having wandered since, round the earth having wandered,
Now I face home again, very pleased and joyous.
(But where is what I started for so long ago?
And why is it yet unfound?)"

* * *

"I know I am deathless.
I know that this orbit of mine cannot be swept by a carpenter's compass;
And whether I come to my own to-day, or in ten thousand or ten million years,

I can cheerfully take it now or with equal cheerfulness can wait."

* * *

"As to you, Life, I reckon you are the leavings of many deaths.
No doubt I have died myself ten thousand times before."

* * *

"Births have brought us richness and variety, and other births have brought us richness and variety."

* * *

And this quotation from the American poet N. P. Willis:

"But what a mystery this erring mind?
It wakes within a frame of various powers
A stranger in a new and wondrous world.
It brings an instinct from some other sphere,
For its fine senses are familiar all,
And with the unconscious habit of a dream
It calls and they obey. The priceless sight
Springs to its curious organ, and the ear
Learns strangely to detect the articulate air
In its unseen divisions, and the tongue
Gets its miraculous lesson with the rest,
And in the midst of an obedient throng
Of well trained ministers, the mind goes forth
To search the secrets of its new found home."

Looked eerily at each other in mutual [illegible] and wit.

As to your data, I [illegible] you are [illegible] bearings of many words.

No [illegible] I [illegible] myself ten thousand miles [illegible]

But the [illegible] [illegible] and variety, and other [illegible] us [illegible] and variety.

And this quotation from the American poet, [illegible] Whittier:

But what a mystery this erring mind?
It wakes within a frame [illegible]—as [illegible]
A stranger in a new and wondrous world.
It [illegible] an [illegible] [illegible]
Its [illegible] are familiar all.
And with the unconscious habit of a dream
It calls and is obeyed. The powers, its slaves
Spring to its [illegible]
[illegible]
[illegible]
[illegible]
And [illegible] through
Of [illegible], the hand does for
[illegible]"

THE TENTH LESSON

Spiritual Evolution.

One of the things that repel many persons who have had their attention directed to the subject of Metempsychosis for the first time, is the idea that they have evolved *as a soul* from individual lowly forms, for instance that they have at one time been an individual plant, and then an individual animal form, and then an individual higher animal form, and so on until now they are the particular individual human form contemplating the subject. This idea, which has been taught by many teachers, is repellent to the average mind, for obvious reasons, and naturally so, for it has no foundation in truth.

While this lesson is principally concerned with the subject of the Spiritual Evolution of the human soul, since it became a human soul, still it may be as well to mention the previous phase of evolution, briefly, in order to prevent misconception, and to dispel previously acquired error.

The atom, although it possesses life and a certain degree of mind, and acts as an individual temporarily, has no permanent individuality that reincarnates. When the atom is evolved it becomes a centre of energy in the great atomic principle, and when it is finally dissolved it resolves itself back into its original state, and its life as an individual atom ceases, although the experience it has gained becomes the property of the entire principle. It is as if a body of water were to be resolved into millions of tiny dew-drops for a time, and each dew-drop was then to acquire certain outside material in solution. In that case, each dew-drop when it again returned to the body of water, would carry with it its foreign material, which would become the property of the whole. And subsequently formed dew-drops would carry in their substance a particle of the foreign matter brought back home by the previous generation of dew-drops, and would thus be a little different from their predecessors. And this process, continuing for many generations of dew-drops, would ultimately cause the greatest changes in the composition of the successive generations.

This, in short, is the story of the change and improving forms of life. From the atoms into the elements; from the lower elements into those forming protoplasm; from the protoplasm to the lower forms of animal life; from these lower forms on to higher forms —this is the story. But it is all a counterpart of the dew-drop and the body of water, *until the human soul is evolved.*

The plants and the lower forms of animal life are not permanent individual souls, but each family is a *group-soul* corresponding to the body of water from which the dew-drop arose. From these family group-souls gradually break off minor groups, representing species, and so on into sub-species. At last when the forms reach the plane of man, the group-soul breaks itself up into *permanent individual souls,* and true Metempsychosis begins. That is, *each individual human soul becomes a permanent individual entity,* destined to evolve and perfect itself along the lines of spiritual evolution.

And from this point begins our story of Spiritual Evolution.

The story of Man, the Individual, begins amidst humble surroundings. Primitive man, but little above the level of the lower animals in point of intelligence, has nevertheless that distinguishing mark of Individuality—"Self-Consciousness," which is the demarkation between Beast and Man. And even the lowest of the lowest races had at least a "trace" of this Self-Consciousness, which made of them individuals, and caused the fragment of the race-soul to separate itself from the general principle animating the race, and to fasten its "I" conscious upon itself, rather than upon the underlying race-soul, along instinctive lines. Do you know just what this Self-Consciousness is, and how it differs from the Physical Consciousness of the lower animals? Perhaps we had better pause a moment to consider it at this place.

The lower animals are of course conscious of the bodies, and their wants, feelings, emotions, desires, etc., and their actions are in response to the animating impulses coming from this plane of consciousness. But it stops there. They "know," but they do not "know that they know"; that is, they have not yet arrived at a state in which they can think of themselves as "I," and to reason upon their thoughts and mental operations. It is like the consciousness of a very young child, which feels and knows its sensations and wants, but is unable to think of itself as "I," and to turn the mental gaze inward. In another book of these series, we have used the illustration of the horse which has been left standing out in the cold sleet and rain, and which undoubtedly feels and knows the unpleasant sensations arising therefrom, and longs to get away from the unpleasant environment. But, still, he is unable to analyze his mental states and wonder whether his master will come out to him soon, or think how cruel it is to keep him out of his warm comfortable stable; or wonder whether he will be taken out in the cold rain again tomorrow; or feel envious of other horses who are indoors; or wonder why he is kept out cold nights, etc., etc. In short, the horse is unable to think as would a reasoning man under just the same circumstances. He is aware of the discomfort, just as would be the man; and he would run away home, if he were able, just as would the man. But he is not able to pity himself, nor to think about his personality, as would a man—he is not able to wonder whether life is worth the living, etc., as would a man. He "knows" but is not able to reflect upon the "knowing."

In the above illustration, the principal point is that the horse does not "know himself" as an entity, while even the most primitive man is able to so recognize himself as an "I." If the horse were able to think in words, he would think "feel," "cold," "hurt," etc., but he would be unable to think "*I* feel; *I* am cold; *I* am hurt," etc. The thought "I" would be missing.

It is true that the "I" consciousness of the primitive

man was slight, and was but a degree above the Physical Consciousness of the higher apes, but nevertheless it had sprung into being, never again to be lost. The primitive man was like a child a few years old—he was able to say "I," and to think "I." *He had become an individual soul.*

And this individual soul inhabited and animated a body but little removed from that of an ape. But this new consciousness began to mould that rude body and the ascent was begun. Each generation showed a physical improvement over that of the preceding one, according to the lines of physical evolution, and as the developing soul demanded more perfect and developed bodies the bodies were evolved to meet the demand, for the mental demand has ever been the cause of the physical form.

The soul of the primitive man reincarnated almost immediately after the death of the physical body, because the experiences gained were mostly along the lines of the physical, the mental planes being scarcely brought into play, while the higher and spiritual faculties were almost entirely obscured from sight. Life after life the soul of the primitive man lived out in rapid succession. But in each new embodiment there was a slight advance over that of the previous one. Experience, or rather the result of experiences, were carried over, and profited by. New lessons were learned and unlearned, improved upon or discarded. And the race grew and unfolded.

After a time the number of advancing souls which

had outstripped their fellows in progress became sufficiently large for sub-races to be formed, and so the branching off process began. In this way the various races and types were formed, and the progress of Mankind gained headway. At this point we may as well consider the history of the Races of Mankind, that we may see how the great tide-wave of Soul has ever pressed onward, marking higher and still higher stages of progress, and also how the various minor waves of the great wave pushed in and then receded, only to be followed by still higher waves. The story is most interesting.

The Yogi Teachings inform us that the Grand Cycle of Man's Life on the Earth is composed of Seven Cycles, of which we are now living in the third-seventh part of the Fifth Cycle. These Cycles may be spoken of as the Great Earth Periods, separated from each other by some great natural cataclysm which destroyed the works of the previous races of men, and which started afresh the progress called "civilization," which, as all students know, manifests a rise and fall like unto that of the tides.

Man in the First Cycle emerged from a gross animal-like state into a condition somewhat advanced. It was a slow progress, but nevertheless a distinct series of advances were made by the more progressive souls who passed over on to the Second Cycle, embodying themselves as the ruling races in the same, their less progressive brothers incarnating in the lower tribes of the Second Cycle. It must be remembered that the souls which do not advance during a Cycle reincarnate in the next Cycle among the lower races. So that even in this Fifth Cycle we have remnants of the previous cycles, the lives of the members of which give us an idea of what life in the earlier cycles must have been.

The Yogi Teachings give us but little information regarding the people of the First and Second Cycles, because of the low state of these ages. The tale, if told, would be the story of the Cave-dweller, and Stone-age people; the Fire-peoples, and all the rest of savage, barbarian crew; there was but little trace of anything like that which we call "civilization," although in the latter periods of the Second Cycle the foundations for the coming civilizations were firmly laid.

After the cataclysm which destroyed the works of Man of the Second Cycle, and left the survivors scattered or disorganized, awaiting the touch of the organizing urge which followed shortly afterward, there dawned the first period of the Third Cycle. The scene of the life of the Third Cycle was laid in what is known to Occultists as Lemuria. Lemuria was a mighty continent situated in what is now known as the Pacific Ocean, and parts of the Indian Ocean. It included Australia, Australasia, and other portions of the Pacific islands, which are in fact surviving portions of the great continent of Lemuria, its highest points, the lower portion having sunk beneath the seas ages and ages ago.

Life in Lemuria is described as being principally concerned with the physical senses, and sensual enjoyment, only a few developed souls having broken through the fetters of materiality and reached the beginnings of the mental and spiritual planes of life. Some few indeed made great progress and were saved from the general wreck, in order to become the leaven which would lighten the mass of mankind during the next Cycle. These developed souls were the teachers of the new races, and were looked upon by the latter as gods and supernatural beings, and legends and traditions concerning them are still existent among the ancient peoples of our present day. Many of the myths of the ancient peoples arose in this way.

The Yogi traditions hold that just prior to the great cataclysm which destroyed the races of the Second Cycle, there was a body of the Chosen Ones which migrated from Lemuria to certain islands of the sea which are now part of the main land of India. These people formed the nucleus of the Occult Teachings of the Lemurians, and developed into the Fount of Truth which has been flowing ever since throughout the successive periods and cycles.

When Lemuria passed away, there arose from the depths of the ocean the continent which was to be the scene of the life and civilization of the Fourth Cycle—the continent of Atlantis. Atlantis was situated in a portion of what is now known as the Atlantic Ocean, beginning at what is now known as the Caribbean Sea and extending over to the region of what is now known as Africa. What are now known as Cuba and the West Indies were among the highest points of the continent, and now stand like monuments to its departed greatness.

The civilization of Atlantis was remarkable, and its people attained heights which seem almost incredible to even those who are familiar with the highest achievements of man in our own times. The Chosen Ones preserved from the cataclysm which destroyed Lemuria, and who lived to a remarkably old age, had stored up within their minds the wisdom and learning of the races that had been destroyed, and they thus gave the Atlanteans an enormous starting-advantage. They soon attained great advancement along all the lines of human endeavor. They perfected mechanical inventions and appliances, reaching far ahead of even our present attainments. In the field of electricity especially they reached the stages that our present races will reach in about two or three hundred years from now. Along the lines of Occult Attainment their progress was far beyond the dreams of the average man of our own race, and in fact from this arose one of the causes of their downfall, for they prostituted the power to base and selfish uses, and Black Magic.

And, so the decline of Atlantis began. But the end did not come at once, or suddenly, but gradually. The continent, and its surrounding islands gradually sank beneath the waves of the Atlantic Ocean, the process occupying over 10,000 years. The Greeks and Romans of our own Cycle had traditions regarding the sinking of the continent, but their knowledge referred only to the disappearance of the small remainder—certain islands—the continent itself having disappeared thousands of years before their time. It is recorded that the Egyptian priests had traditions that the continent itself had disappeared nine thousand years before their time. As was the case with the Chosen Ones of Lemuria, so was it with the Elect of Atlantis, who were taken away from the doomed land some time prior to its destruction. The few advanced people left their homes and migrated to portions of what are now South America and Central America, but which were then islands of the sea. These people have left their traces of their civilization and works, which our antiquaries are discovering to-day.

When the Fifth Cycle dawned (our own cycle, remember) these brave and advanced souls acted as the race-teachers and became as "gods" to those who came afterward. The races were very prolific, and multiplied very rapidly under the most favorable conditions. The souls of the Atlanteans were pressing forward for embodiment, and human forms were born to supply the demand. And now begins the history of our own Cycle—the Fifth Cycle.

But before we begin a consideration of the Fifth Cycle, let us consider for a moment a few points about the laws operating to cause these great changes.

In the first place, each Cycle has a different theatre for its work and action. The continent of Lemuria was not in existence during the Second Cycle, and arose from the ocean bed only when its appointed time came. And, likewise the continent of Atlantis reposed beneath the waves while the Lemurian races manifested during the Third Cycle, rising by means of a convulsion of the earth's surface to play its part during its own period—the Fourth Cycle—only to sink again beneath the waves to make way for the birth of the Fifth Cycle with its races. By means of these cataclysms the races of each Cycle were wiped out when the time came, the few Elect or Chosen ones, that is those who have manifested the right to live on, being carried away to some favorable environment where they became as leaven to the mass—as "gods" to the new races that quickly appear.

It must be remembered, however, that these Chosen Ones are not the only ones saved from the destruction that overtakes the majority of the race. On the contrary a few survivors are preserved, although driven away from their former homes, and reduced to "first principles of living" in order to become the parents of the new races. The new races springing from the fittest of these survivors quickly form sub-races, being composed of the better adapted souls seeking reincarnation, while the less fit sink into barbarism, and show evidences of decay, although a remnant drags on for thousands of years, being composed of the souls of those who have not advanced sufficiently to take a part in the life of the new races. These "left-overs" are in evidence in our own times in the cases of the Australian savages, and some of the African tribes, as well as among the Digger Indians and others of similar grade of intelligence.

In order to understand the advance of each race it must be remembered that the more advanced souls, after passing out of the body, have a much longer period of rest in the higher planes, and consequently do not present themselves for reincarnation until a period quite late when compared with the hasty reincarnation of the less advanced souls who are hurried back to rebirth by reason of the strong earthly attachments and desires. In this way it happens that the earlier races of each Cycle are more primitive folk than those who follow them as the years roll by. The soul of an earth-bound person reincarnates in a few years, and sometimes in a few days, while the soul of an advanced man may repose and rest on the higher planes for centuries—nay, even for thousands of years, until the earth has reached a stage in which the appropriate environment may be afforded it.

Observers, unconnected with Occultism, have noted certain laws which seem to regulate the rise and fall of nations—the procession of ruling races. They do not understand the law of Metempsychosis that alone gives the key to the problem, but nevertheless they have not failed to record the existence of the laws themselves. In order to show that these laws are recognized by persons who are not at all influenced by the Occult Teachings, we take the liberty of quoting from Draper's "History of the Intellectual Development of Europe."

Dr. Draper writes as follows: "We are, as we often say, the creatures of circumstances. In that expression there is a higher philosophy than might at first appear. From this more accurate point of view we should therefore consider the course of these events, recognizing the principle that the affairs of men pass forward in a determinate way, expanding and unfolding themselves. And hence we see that the things of which we have spoken as if they were matters of choice, were in reality forced upon their apparent authors by the necessity of the times. But in truth they should be considered as the presentation of a certain phase of life which nations in their onward course sooner or later assume. To the individual, how well we know that a sober moderation of action, an appropriate gravity of demeanor, belonging to the mature period of life, change from the wanton wilfulness of youth, which may be ushered in, or its beginnings marked by many accidental incidents; in one perhaps by domestic bereavements, in another by the loss of fortune, in a third by ill-health. We are correct enough in imputing to such trials the change of character; but we never deceive ourselves by supposing that it would have failed to take place had these incidents not occurred. There runs an irresistible destiny in the midst of these vicissitudes. There are analogies between the life of a nation, and that of an individual, who, though he may be in one respect the maker of his own fortunes, for happiness or for misery, for good or for evil, though he remains here or goes there as his inclinations prompt, though he does this or abstains from that as he chooses, is nevertheless held fast by an inexorable fate—a fate which brought him into the world involuntarily, so far as he was concerned, which presses him forward through a definite career, the stages of which are absolutely invariable,—infancy, childhood, youth, maturity, old age, with all their characteristic actions and passions, —and which removes him from the scene at the appointed time, in most cases against his will. So also is it with nations; the voluntary is only the outward semblance, covering but hardly hiding the predetermined. Over the events of life we may have control, but none whatever over the law of its progress. There is a geometry that applies to nations an equation of their curve of advance. That no mortal man can touch."

This remarkable passage, just quoted, shows how the close observers of history note the rise and fall of the tides of human race progress, although ignorant of the real underlying causing energy or force. A study of the Occult Teachings alone gives one the hidden secret of human actions and throws the bright light of Truth upon the dark corners of phenomena.

At the beginning of the Fifth Cycle (which is the present one), there were not only the beginnings of the new races which always spring up at the beginning of each new cycle and which are the foundations for the coming races which take advantage of the fresh conditions and opportunities for growth and development

—but there were also the descendants of the Elect saved from the destruction of Atlantis by having been led away and colonized far from the scene of danger. The new races were the descendant of the scattered survivors of the Atlantean peoples, that is, the common run of people of the time. But the Elect few were very superior people, and imparted to their descendants their knowledge and wisdom. So that we see at the beginning of the Fifth Cycle hordes of new, primitive people in certain lands, and in other places advanced nations like the ancestors of the Ancient Egyptians, Persians, Chaldeans, Hindus, etc.

These advanced races were old souls—advanced souls—the progressed and developed souls of Ancient Lemuria and Atlantis, who lived their lives and who are now either on higher planes of life, or else are among us to-day taking a leading part in the world's affairs, striving mightily to save the present races from the misfortunes which overtook their predecessors.

The descendants of the people were the Assyrians and Babylonians. In due time the primitive new races developed and the great Roman, Grecian, and Carthaginian peoples appeared. Then came the rise of other peoples and nations down to the present time. Each race or nation has its rise, its height of attainment, and its decline. When a nation begins to decline it is because its more advanced souls have passed on, and only the less progressive souls are left. The history of all nations show the truth of the Occult

Teachings in this respect, and the strange phenomena noted by historians is explainable in no other way.

It will be seen by the careful student that the Great Law of Metempsychosis is ever urging on humanity toward higher and higher achievements. The advanced souls of a race pass on to new scenes of activity, and even the backward ones are not suffered to lag behind very long, for the continual change, and creation of new environments for them tend to reawaken sleeping energy and to stimulate the lagging one to fresh endeavor and activity. In this way the whole race is being constantly stimulated toward the advancement which is its natural heritage.

But it must not be forgotten that increased power, wisdom and opportunity bring with them increased responsibility. As the soul advances along the lines of Spiritual Evolution, it becomes endowed with a greater and greater opportunity of choosing between the Good and the Evil. In the earlier races the soul was not sufficiently developed to exercise this power of discrimination and choice, and consequently its responsibility was limited. But as the soul advanced and attained greater powers, greater things are expected of it. Power brings with it responsibilities.

The present stage of Man's Spiritual Evolution is a critical one. Men are beginning to be conscious of the great spiritual questions presenting themselves before them for settlement, discrimination and choice. It is like the awakening of the child into manhood or womanhood, and the confronting of problems heretofore undreamt of. Man is developing latent faculties which are bringing to him new perceptions of the Great Truths of Existence, and he can no longer plead "I do not know." In the present stage of life on this planet there is a battle royal being waged between the forces of Materiality and Spirituality, and all are taking part in that battle. Some are ranged on one side, and some on the other, and families are divided over the great question of Spirituality vs. Carnality. But the outcome is in no danger. The Higher will always triumph over the Lower.

On the one side are seen the great mass of men who look upon this present physical life as the only real one, and who regard all ideas of future existence and life as "moonshine" and "wishy-washy talk." These people devote their entire time to the satisfaction of sensual appetites, and the gratification of the lower instincts of the Instinctive Mind. Some few have acquired the Pride of Intellect, and forget the lower physical satisfaction in the greater satisfaction that comes from the exercise of the rational faculties of the mind. But, alas only a few, comparatively, realize the meaning of the word "Spirituality," and know it to be a thing of Strength rather than of Weakness. But even these few are the leaven that shall lighten the mass of the race in due time. Even now the evidences of the work of those who have attained Spiritual Consciousness is being manifested. On all sides one may see signs of spiritual unrest and distress affecting even those who know not the meaning of the term. Men are forsaking old ideals, creeds and dogmas, and are running hither and thither seeking something they feel to be necessary, but of the nature of which they know nothing. They are feeling the hunger for Peace—the thirst for Knowledge—and they are seeking satisfaction in all directions.

This is not only the inevitable working of the Law of Evolution, but is also a manifestation of the power and love of the great souls that have passed on to higher planes of existence, and who have become as angels and arch-angels. These beings are filled with the love of the race, and are setting into motion influences that are being manifest in many directions, the tendency of which are to bring the race to a realization of its higher power, faculties, and destiny.

As we have said in other places, one of the greatest difficulties in the way of the seeker after Truth in his consideration of the question of Spiritual Evolution is the feeling that rebirth is being forced upon him, without any say on his part, and against his desires. But this is far from being correct. It is true that the whole process is according to the Great Law, but that Law operates through the force of Desire and Attraction. The soul is attracted toward rebirth by reason of its desire or rather the essence of its desires. It is reborn only because it has within itself the desire for further experience, and opportunity for unfoldment. And it is reborn into certain environments solely because it has within itself unsatisfied desires for those environments, etc. The process is just as regular and scientific as is the attraction of one atom of matter for another.

Each soul has within itself certain elements of desire and attraction, and it attracts to itself certain conditions and experiences, and is in turn attracted by these things. This is the law of life, in the body and out of it. And there is no injustice in the law—it is the essence of justice itself, for it gives to each just what is required to fill the indwelling desires, or else the conditions and experiences designed to burn out the desires which are holding one back, and the destruction of which will make possible future advancement.

For instance, if one is bound by the inordinate desire for material wealth, the Law of Karma will attract him to a rebirth in conditions in which he will be surrounded by wealth and luxury until he becomes sickened with them and will find his heart filled with the desire to flee from them and toward higher and more satisfying things. Of course the Law of Karma acts in other ways, as we shall see in our next lesson—it deals with one's debts and obligations, also. The Law of Karma is closely connected with Metempsychosis, and one must be considered in connection with the other, always.

Not only is it true that man's rebirths are in strict accordance with the law of Attraction and Desire, but it is also true that after he attains a certain stage of spiritual unfoldment he enters into the conscious stage of rebirth and thereafter he is reborn consciously and with full foreknowledge. Many are now entering into this stage of development, and have a partial consciousness of their past lives, which also implies that they have had at least a partial consciousness of approaching rebirth, for the two phases of consciousness run together.

Those individuals of a race who have outstripped their fellows in spiritual unfoldment, are still bound by the Karma of the particular race to which they belong, up to a certain point. And as the entire race, or at least a large proportion of it, must move forward as a whole, such individuals must needs wait also. But they are not compelled to suffer a tiresome round of continued rebirths amid environments and conditions which they have outgrown. On the contrary, the advanced individual soul is allowed to wait until the race reaches its own stage of advancement, when it again joins in the upward movement, in full consciousness, however. In the interim he may pass his well earned rest either on some of the higher planes of rest, or else in conscious temporary sojourn in other material spheres helping in the great work as a Teacher and worker for Good and Spiritual Evolution among those who need such help. In fact there are in the world to-day, individual souls which have reached similar stages on other planets, and who are spending their rest period here amidst the comparatively lower Earth conditions, striving to lift up the Earth souls to greater heights.

So long as people allow themselves to become attached to material objects, so long will they be reborn in conditions in which these objects bind them fast. It is only when the soul frees itself from these entangling obstructions that it is born in conditions of freedom. Some outgrow these material attachments by right thinking and reasoning, while others seem to be compelled to live them out, and thus outlive them, before they are free. At last when the soul realizes that these things are merely incidents of the lower personality, and have naught to do with the real individuality, then, and then only, do they fall from it like a wornout cloak, and are left behind while it bounds forward on The Path fresh from the lighter weight being carried.

The Yogi Philosophy teaches that Man will live forever, ascending from higher to higher planes, and then on and on and on. Death is but the physical symbol of a period of Soul Rest, similar to sleep of the tired body, and is just as much to be welcomed and greeted with thanks. Life is continuous, and its object is development, unfoldment and growth. We are in Eternity now as much as we ever shall be. Our souls may exist out of the body as well as in it, although bodily incarnation is necessary at this stage of our development. As we progress on to higher planes of life, we shall incarnate in bodies far more ethereal than those now used by us, just as in the past we used bodies almost incredibly grosser and coarser than those we call our own to-day. Life is far more than a thing of three-score and ten years—it is really a succession of such lives, on an ascending scale, that which we call our personal self to-day being merely the essence of the experiences of countless lives in the past.

The Soul is working steadily upward, from higher to higher, from gross to finer forms and manifestations. And it will steadily work for ages to come, always progressing, always advancing, always unfolding. The Universe contains many worlds for the Soul to inhabit, and then after it has passed on to other Universes, there will still be Infinitude before it. The destiny of the Soul of Man is of wondrous promise and possibilities—the mind to-day cannot begin to even dream of what is before the Soul. Those who have already advanced many steps beyond you—those Elder Brethren—are constantly extending to you aid in many directions. They are extending to you the Unseen Hand, which lifts you over many a hard place and dangerous crossing—but you recognize it not except in a vague way. There are now in existence, on planes infinitely higher than your own, intelligences of transcendent glory and magnificence—but they were once Men even as you are to-day. They have so far progressed upon the Path that they have become as angels and archangels when compared with you. And, blessed thought, even as these exalted ones were once even as you, so shall you, in due course of Spiritual Evolution, become even as these mighty ones.

The Yogi Philosophy teaches that You who are reading these lines have lived many lives previous to the present one. You have lived in the lower forms, and have worked your way arduously along the Path until now you are reaching the stage of Spiritual Consciousness in which the past and future will begin to appear plain to you for the first time. You have lived as the cave-man—the cliff-dweller—the savage—the barbarian. You have been the warrior—the priest—the Medieval scholar and occultist—the prince—the pauper. You have lived in Lemuria—in Atlantis—in India—in Persia—in Egypt—in ancient Rome and Greece—and are now playing your part in the Western civilization, associating with many with whom you have had relations in your past lives.

In closing this lesson, let us quote from a previous writing from the same pen that writes this lesson:

"Toward what goal is all this Spiritual Evolution tending? What does it all mean? From the low planes of life to the highest—all are on The Path. To what state or place does The Path lead? Let us attempt to answer by asking you to imagine a series of millions of circles, one within the other. Each circle means a stage of Life. The outer circles are filled with life in its lowest and most material stages—each circle nearer the Centre holds higher and higher forms—until Men (or what were once Men) become as gods. Still on, and on, and on, does the form of life grow higher, until the human mind cannot grasp the idea. But what is the Centre? The MIND of the entire Spiritual Body—the ABSOLUTE! And we are traveling toward that Centre!"

And again from the same source:

"But beyond your plane, and beyond mine, are plane after plane, connected with our earth, the splendors of which man cannot conceive. And there are likewise many planes around the other planets of our chain—and there are millions of other worlds—and there are chains of universes just as there are chains of planets—and then greater groups of these chains—and so on greater and grander beyond the power of man to imagine—on and on and on and on—higher and higher—to inconceivable heights. An infinity of infinities of worlds are before us. Our world and our planetary system and our system of suns, and our system of solar systems, are but as grains of sand on the beach of the mighty ocean. But then you cry, 'But what am I—poor mortal thing—lost among all this inconceivable greatness?' The answer comes that You are that most precious thing—a living soul. And if you were destroyed the whole system of universes would crumble, for you are as necessary as the greatest part of it—it cannot do without you—you cannot be lost or destroyed—you are a part of it all, and are eternal. 'But,' you ask, 'beyond all of this of which you have told me, what is there—what is the Centre of it All?' Your Teacher's face takes on a rapt expression—a light not of earth beams forth from his countenance. *'THE ABSOLUTE!'* he replies.

THE ELEVENTH LESSON.

The Law of Karma.

"Karma" is a Sanscrit term for that great Law known to Western thinkers as Spiritual Cause and Effect, or Causation. It relates to the complicated affinities for either good or evil that have been acquired by the soul throughout its many incarnations. These affinities manifest as characteristics enduring from one incarnation to another, being added to here, softened or altered there, but always pressing forward for expression and manifestation. And, so, it follows that what each one of us is in this life depends upon is what we have been and how we have acted in our past lives.

Throughout the operations of the Law of Karma the manifestation of Perfect Justice is apparent. We are not punished *for* our sins, as the current beliefs have it, but instead we are punished *by* our sins. We are not rewarded *for* our good acts, but we received our reward *through and by* characteristics, qualities, affinities, etc., acquired by reason of our having performed these good acts in previous lives. We are our own judges and executioners. In our present lives we are storing up good or bad Karma which will stick to us closely, and which will demand expression and manifestation in lives to come. When we fasten around ourselves the evil of bad Karma, we have taken to shelter a monster which will gnaw into our very vitals until we shake him off by developing opposite qualities. And when we draw to ourselves the good Karma of Duty well performed, kindness well expressed, and Good Deeds freely performed without hope of reward, then do we weave for ourselves the beautiful garments which we are destined to wear upon the occasion of our future lives.

The Yogi Teachings relating to the Law of Karma do not teach us that Sin is an offense against the Power which brought us into being, so much as it is an offense against ourselves. We cannot injure the Absolute, nor harm It in any way. But we may harm each other, and in so doing harm ourselves. The Yogis teach that Sin is largely a matter of ignorance and misunderstanding of our true nature, and that the lesson must be well learned until we are able to see the folly and error of our former course, and thus are able to remedy our past errors and to avoid their recurrence. By Karma the effects arising from our sins cling to us, until we become sick and weary of them, and seek their cause in our hearts. When we have discovered the evil cause of these effects, we learn to hate it and tear it from us as a foul thing, and are thence evermore relieved of it.

The Yogis view the sinning soul as the parent does the child who will persist in playing with forbidden things. The parent cautions the child against playing with the stove, but still the child persists in its disobedience, and sooner or later receives a burn for its meddling. The burn is not a *punishment* for the disobedience (although it may seem so to it) but comes in obedience to a natural law which is invariable. The child finds out that stoves and burns are connected, and begins to see some sense and reason in the admonitions of the parent. The love of the parent sought to save the child the pain of the burn, and yet the child-nature persisted in experimenting, and was taught the lesson. But the lesson once thoroughly learned, it is not necessary to forbid the child the stove, for it has learned the danger for itself and thereafter avoids it.

And thus it is with the human soul passing on from one life to another. It learns new lessons, gathers new experiences, and learns to recognize the pain that invariably comes from Wrong Action, and the Happiness that invariably comes from Right Action. As it progresses it learns how hurtful certain courses of action are, and like the burnt child it avoids them thereafter.

If we will but stop to consider for a moment the relative degrees of temptation to us and to others, we may see the operations of past Karma in former lives. Why is it that this thing is "no temptation" to you, while it is the greatest temptation to another. Why is it that certain things do not seem to have any attraction for him, and yet they attract you so much that you have to use all of your will power to resist them? It is because of the Karma in your past lives. The things that do not now tempt you, have been outlived in some former life, and you have profited by your own experiences, or those of others, or else through some teaching given you by one who had been attracted to you by your unfolding consciousness of Truth.

We are profiting to-day by the lessons of our past lives. If we have learned them well we are receiving the benefit, while if we have turned our backs on the words of wisdom offered us, or have refused to learn the lesson perfectly, we are compelled to sit on the same old school-benches and hear the same old lesson repeated until it is fairly driven into our consciousness. We wonder why it is that other persons can perform certain evil acts that seem so repulsive to us, and are apt to pride ourselves upon our superior virtue. But those who know, realize that their unfortunate brethren have not paid sufficient attention to the lesson of the past, and are having it repeated to them in a more drastic form this time. They know that the virtuous ones are simply reaping the benefit of their own application in the past, but that their lesson is not over, and that unless they advance and hold fast to that which they have attained, as well, they will be outstripped by many of those whose failure they are now viewing with wonder and scorn.

It is hard for us to fully realize that we are what we are because of our past experiences. It is difficult for us to value the experiences that we are now going through, because we do not fully appreciate the value of bitter experiences once lived out and outlived. Let us look back over the experiences of this present life. for instance. How many bitter episodes are there which we wish had never happened, and how we wish we could tear them out of our consciousness. But we do not realize that from these same bitter experiences came knowledge and wisdom that we would not part with under any circumstances. And yet if we were to tear away from us the cause of these benefits, we would tear away the benefits also, and would find ourselves back just where we were before the experience happened to us. What we would like to do is to hold on to the benefits that came from the experience—the knowledge and wisdom that were picked from the tree of pain. But we cannot separate the effect from the cause in this way, and must learn to look back upon these bitter experiences as the causes from which our present knowledge, wisdom and attainment proceeded. Then may we cease to hate these things, and to see that good may come from evil, under the workings of the Law.

And when we are able to do this, we shall be able to regard the painful experiences of our present day as the inevitable outcome of causes away back in our past, but which will work surely toward increased knowledge, wisdom and attainment, if we will but see the Good underlying the working of the Law. When we fall in with the working of the Law of Karma we recognize its pain not as an injustice or punishment, but as the beneficent operation of a Law which, although apparently working Evil, has for its end and aim Ultimate Good.

Many object to the teachings of the Law of Karma by saying that the experiences of each life, not being remembered, must be useless and without value. This is a very foolish position to take concerning the matter. These experiences although not fully remembered, are not lost to us at all—they are made a part of the material of which our minds are composed. They exist in the form of feelings, characteristics, inclinations, likes and dislikes, affinities, attractions, repulsions, etc., etc., and are as much in evidence as are the experiences of yesterday which are fresh in our memory. Look back over your present life, and try to remember the experiences of the past years. You will find that you remember but few of the events of your life. The pressing and constant experiences of each of the days that you have lived have been, for the most part, forgotten. Though these experiences may have seemed very vivid and real to you when they occurred, still they have faded into nothingness now, and they are to all intents and purposes *lost* to you. But *are* they lost? Not at all. You are what you are because of the results of these experiences. Your character has been moulded and shaped, little by little, by these apparently forgotten pains, pleasures, sorrows and happinesses. This trial strengthened you along certain lines; that one changed your point of view and made you see things with a broader sweep of vision. This grief caused you to feel the pain of others; that disappointment spurred you on to new endeavors. And each and every one of them left a permanent mark upon your personality—upon your character. All men are what they are by reason of what they have lived through and out. And though these happenings, scenes, circumstances, occurrences, experiences, have faded from the memory, their effects are indelibly imprinted upon the fabric of the character, and the man of to-day is different from what he would have been had the happening or experience not entered into his life.

And this same rule applies to the characteristics brought over from past incarnations. You have not the memory of the experiences, but you have the fruit in the shape of "characteristics," tastes, inclinations, etc. You have a tendency toward certain things, and a distaste for others. Certain things attract, while others repel you. All of these things are the result of your experiences in former incarnations. Your very taste and inclination toward occult studies which has caused you to read these lessons is your legacy from some former life in which some one spoke a word or two to you regarding the subject, and attracted your interest and desire. You learned some little about the subject then—perhaps much—and developed a desire for more knowledge along these lines, which manifesting in your present life has brought you in contact with further instruction. The same inclination will lead to further advancement in this life, and still greater opportunities in future incarnations. Nearly every one who reads these lines has felt that much of this occult instruction imparted is but a "re-learning" of something previously known, although many of the things taught have never been heard before in this life. You pick up a book and read something, and know at once that it is so, because in some vague way you have a consciousness of having studied and worked out the problem in some past period of your lives. All this is the working of the Law of Karma, which caused you to attract that for which you have an affinity, and which also causes others to be attracted to you.

Many are the reunions of people who have been related to each other in previous lives. The old loves, and old hates work out their Karmic results in our lives. We are bound to those whom we have loved, and also to those whom we may have injured. The story must be worked out to the end, although a knowledge of the Law undoubtedly relieves one of many entangling attachments and Karmic relationships, by pointing out the nature of the relation, and enabling one to free himself mentally from the bond, which process tends to dissolve much of the Karmic entanglements.

Life is a great school for the learning of lessons. It has many grades, many classes, many scales of progress. And the lessons must be learned whether we will or no. If we refuse or neglect to learn the lesson we are sent back to accomplish the task, again and again, until the lesson is finally learned. Nothing once learned is ever forgotten entirely. There is an indelible imprint of the lesson in our character, which manifests as predispositons, tastes, inclinations, etc. All that goes to make up that which we call "Character" is the workings of the Law of Karma. There is no such thing as Chance. Nothing ever "happens." All is regulated by the Law of Cause and Effect or Karma. As a man sows so shall he reap, in a literal sense. You are what you are to-day, by reason of what you were in your last life. And in your next life you will be what you are making of yourself to-day. You are your own judge, and executioner—your own bestower of rewards. But the Love of the Absolute is ever working to lead you upward to the Light, and to open your soul to that knowledge that, in the words of the Yogis, "burns up Karma," and enables you to throw off the burden of Cause and Effect that you have been carrying around with you, and which has weighted you down.

In the Fourteen Lessons we quoted from Mr. Berry Benson, a writer in the *Century Magazine* for May, 1894. The quotation fits so beautifully into this place, that we venture to reproduce it here once more, with your permission. It reads as follows:

"A little boy went to school. He was very little. All that he knew he had drawn in with his mother's milk. His teacher (who was God) placed him in the lowest class, and gave him these lessons to learn: Thou shalt not kill. Thou shalt do no hurt to any living thing. Thou shalt not steal. So the man did not kill; but he was cruel, and he stole. At the end of the day (when his beard was gray—when the night was come) his teacher (who was God) said: Thou hast learned not to kill, but the other lessons thou hast not learned. Come back tomorrow.

"On the morrow he came back a little boy. And his teacher (who was God) put him in a class a little higher, and gave him these lessons to learn: Thou shalt do no hurt to any living thing. Thou shalt not steal. Thou shalt not cheat. So the man did no hurt to any living thing; but he stole and cheated. And at the end of the day (when his beard was gray—when the night was come) his teacher (who was God) said: Thou hast learned to be merciful. But the other lessons thou hast not learned. Come back tomorrow.

"Again, on the morrow, he came back, a little boy. And his teacher (who was God) put him in a class yet a little higher, and gave him these lessons to learn: Thou shalt not steal. Thou shalt not cheat. Thou shalt not covet. So the man did not steal; but he cheated and he coveted. And at the end of the day (when his beard was gray—when the night was come) his teacher (who was God) said: Thou hast learned not to steal. But the other lessons thou hast not learned. Come back, my child, tomorrow.

"This is what I have read in the faces of men and women, in the book of the world, and in the scroll of the heavens, which is writ with stars."

Under the operation of the Law of Karma every man is master of his own destiny—he rewards himself—he punishes himself—he builds, tears down and develops his character, always, however, under the brooding influence of the Absolute which is Love Infinite and which is constantly exerting the upward spiritual urge, which is drawing the soul toward its ultimate haven of rest. Man must, and does, work out his own salvation and destiny, but the upward urge is always there—never tiring—never despairing —knowing always that Ultimate Victory belongs to the soul.

Under the Law of Karma every action, yea, every thought as well, has its Karmic effect upon the future incarnations of the soul. And, not exactly in the nature of punishment or rewards, in the general acceptation of the term, but as the invariable operation of the Law of Cause and Effect. The thoughts of a person are like seeds which seek to press forward into growth, bud, blossom and fruit. Some spring into growth in this life, while others are carried over into future lives. The actions of this life may represent only the partial growth of the thought seed, and future lives may be necessary for its full blossoming and fruition. Of course, the individual who understands the Truth, and who has mentally divorced himself from the fruits of his actions—who has robbed material Desire of its vital force by seeing it as it is, and not as a part of his Real Self—his seed-thoughts do not spring into blossom and fruit in future lives, for he has killed their germ. The Yogis express this thought by the illustration of the baked-seeds. They show their pupils that while ordinary seeds sprout, blossom and bear fruit, still if one bakes the seeds their vitality is gone, and while they may serve the purposes of a nourishing meal still they can never cause sprout, blossom or fruit. Then the pupil is instructed in the nature of Desire, and shown how desires invariably spring into plant, blossom and fruit, the life of the person being the soil in which they flourish. But Desires understood, and set off from the Real Man, are akin to baked-seeds—they have been subjected to the heat of spiritual wisdom and are thus robbed of their vitality, and are unable to bear fruit. In this way the understood and mastered Desire bears no Karmic fruit of future action.

The Yogis teach that there are two great principles at work in the matter of Karmic Law affecting the conditions of rebirth. The first principle is that whereby the prevailing desires, aspirations, likes, and dislikes, loves and hates, attractions and repulsions, etc., press the soul into conditions in which these characteristics may have a favorable and congenial soil for development. The second principle is that which may be spoken of as the urge of the unfolding Spirit, which is always urging forward toward fuller expression, and the breaking down of confining sheaths, and which thus exerts a pressure upon the soul awaiting reincarnation which causes it to seek higher environments and conditions than its desires and aspiration, as well as its general characteristics, would demand. These two apparently conflicting (and yet actually harmonious) principles acting and reacting upon each other, determine the conditions of rebirth, and have a very material effect upon the Karmic Law. One's life is largely a conflict between these two forces, the one tending to hold the soul to the present conditions resulting from past lives, and the other ever at work seeking to uplift and elevate it to greater heights.

The desires and characteristics brought over from the past lives, of course, seek fuller expression and manifestation upon the lines of the past lives. These tendencies simply wish to be let alone and to grow according to their own laws of development and manifestation. But the unfolding Spirit, knowing that the soul's best interests are along the lines of spiritual unfoldment and growth, brings a steady pressure to bear, life after life, upon the soul, causing it to gradually kill out the lower desires and characteristics, and to develop qualities which tend to lead it upward instead of allowing it to remain on its present level, there to bring to blossom and fruit many low thoughts and desires. Absolute Justice reigns over the operations of the Law of Karma, but back of that and superior even to its might is found the Infinite Love of the Absolute which tends to Redeem the race. It is that love that is back of all the upward tendencies of the soul, and which we all feel within our inner selves in our best moments. The light of the Spirit (Love) is ever there.

Our relationship to others in past lives has its effect upon the working of the Law of Karma. If in the past we have formed attachments for other individuals, either through love or hate; either by kindness or cruelty; these attachments manifest in our present life, for these persons are bound to us, and we to them, by the bonds of Karma, until the attachment is worn out. Such people will in the present life have certain relationships to us, the object of which is the working out of the problems in which we are mutually concerned, the adjustment of relationship, the "squaring up" of accounts, the development of both. We are apt to be placed in a position to receive hurts from those whom we have hurt in past lives, and this not through the idea of revenge, but by the inexorable working out of the Law of Compensation in Karmic adjustments. And when we are helped, comforted and receive favors from those who we helped in past lives, it is not merely a reward, but the operation of the same law of Justice. The person who hurts us in this way may have no desire to do so, and may even be distressed because he is used as an instrument in this way, but the Karmic Law places him in a position where he unwittingly and without desire acts so that you receive pain through him. Have you not felt yourselves hurting another, although you had no desire and intention of so doing, and, in fact, were sorely distressed because you could not prevent the pain? This is the operation of Karma. Have you not found yourself placed where you unexpectedly were made the bestower of favors upon some almost unknown persons? This is Karma. The Wheel turns slowly, but it makes the complete circle.

Karma is the companion law to Metempsychosis. The two are inextricably connected, and their operations are closely interwoven. Constant and unvarying in operation, Karma manifests upon and in worlds, planets, races, nations, families and persons. Everywhere in space is the great law in operation in some form. The so-called mechanical operations called Causation are as much a phase of Karma as is the highest phases manifest on the higher planes of life, far beyond our own. And through it all is ever the urge toward perfection—the upward movement of all life. The Yogi teachings regard the Universe as a mighty whole, and the Law of Karma as the one great law operating and manifesting through that whole.

How different is the workings of this mighty Law from the many ideas advanced by man to account for the happenings of life. Mere Chance is no explanation, for the careful thinker must inevitably come to the conclusion that in an Universe governed by Law, there can be no room for Chance. And to suppose that all rewards and punishments are bestowed by a personal deity, in answer to prayers, supplications, good behavior, offerings, etc., is to fall back into the childhood stage of the race thought. The Yogis teach that the sorrow, suffering and affliction witnessed on all sides of us, as well as the joy, happiness and blessings also in evidence, are not caused by the will or whim of some capricious diety to reward his friends and punish his enemies—but by the working of an invariable Law which metes out to each his measure of good and ill according to his Karmic attachments and relationships.

Those who are suffering, and who see no cause for

their pain, are apt to complain and rebel when they see others of no apparent merit enjoying the good things of life which have been denied their apparently more worthy brethren. The churches have no answer except "It is God's will," and that "the Divine motive must not be questioned." These answers seem like mockery, particularly when the idea of Divine Justice is associated with the teaching. There is no other answer compatible with Divine Justice other than the Law of Karma, which makes each person responsible for his or her happiness or misery. And there is nothing so stimulating to one as to know that he has within himself the means to create for himself newer and better conditions of life and environment. We are what we are to-day by reason of what we were in our yesterdays. We will be in our tomorrows that which we have started into operation to-day. As we sow in this life, so shall we reap in the next—we are now reaping that which we have sown in the past. St. Paul voiced a world truth when he said: "Brethren, be not deceived. God is not mocked, for whatsoever a man soweth that shall he also reap."

The teachers divide the operation of Karma into three general classes, as follows:

(1) The Karmic manifestations which are now under way in our lives, producing results which are the effects of causes set into motion in our past lives. This is the most common form, and best known phase of Karmic manifestation.

(2) The Karma which we are now acquiring and

storing up by reason of our actions, deeds, thoughts and mental and spiritual relationships. This stored up Karma will spring into operation in future lives, when the body and environments appropriate for its manifestation presents itself or is secured; or else when other Karma tending to restrict its operations is removed. But one does not necessarily have to wait until a future life in order to set into operation and manifestation the Karma of the present life. For there come times in which there being no obstructing Karma brought over from a past life, the present life Karma may begin to manifest.

(3) The Karma brought over from past incarnations, which is not able to manifest at the present time owing to the opposition presented by other Karma of an opposite nature, serves to hold the first in check. It is a well known physical law, which likewise manifests on the mental plane, that two opposing forces result in neutralization, that is, both of the forces are held in check. Of course, though, a more powerful Karma may manage to operate, while a weaker is held in check by it.

Not only have individuals their own Karma, but families, races, nations and worlds have their collective Karma. In the cases of races, if the race Karma generated in the past be favorable on the whole, the race flourishes and its influence widens. If on the contrary its collective Karma be bad, the race gradually disappears from the face of the earth, the souls constituting it separating according to their

Karmic attractions, some going to this race and some to another. Nations are bound by their Karma, as any student of history may perceive if he studies closely the tides of national progress or decline.

The Karma of a nation is made up of the collective Karma of the individuals composing it, so far as their thoughts and acts have to do with the national spirit and acts. Nations as nations cease to exist, but the souls of the individuals composing them still live on and make their influence felt in new races, scenes and environments. The ancient Egyptians, Persians, Medes, Chaldeans, Romans, Grecians and many other ancient races have disappeared, but their reincarnating souls are with us to-day. The modern revival of Occultism is caused by an influx of the souls of these old peoples pouring in on the Western worlds.

The following quotation from *The Secret Doctrine,* that remarkable piece of occult literature, will be interesting at this point:

"Nor would the ways of Karma be inscrutable were men to work in union and harmony instead of disunion and strife. For our ignorance of those ways—which one portion of mankind calls the ways of Providence, dark and intricate, while another sees in them the action of blind fatalism, and a third simple Chance with neither gods nor devils to guide them—would surely disappear if we would but attribute all these to their correct cause. With right knowledge, or at any rate with a confident conviction that our neighbors will no more work harm to us than we would think of harming them, two-thirds of the world's evil would vanish into thin air. Were no man to hurt his brother, Karma-Nemesis would have neither cause to work for, nor weapons to act through. . . . We cut these numerous windings in our destinies daily with our own hands, while we imagine that we are pursuing a track on the royal road of respectability and duty, and then complain of those ways being so intricate and so dark. We stand bewildered before the mystery of our own making and the riddles of life that we will not solve, and then accuse the great Sphinx of devouring us. But verily there is not an accident in our lives, not a misshapen day or a misfortune, that could not be traced back to our own doings in this or another life. . . . Knowledge of Karma gives the conviction that if—

> 'Virtue in distress and vice in triumph
> Makes atheists of Mankind,'

it is only because that mankind has ever shut its eyes to the great truth that man is himself his own savior as his own destroyer; that he need not accuse heaven, and the gods, fates and providence, of the apparent injustice that reigns in the midst of humanity. But let him rather remember that bit of Grecian wisdom which warns man to forbear accusing THAT which 'Just though mysterious, leads us on unerring
Through ways unmarked from guilt to punishment'
—which are now the ways and the high road on which move onward the great European nations. The Western Aryans have every nation and tribe like their

eastern brethren of the fifth race, their Golden and their Iron ages, their period of comparative irresponsibility, or the Satya age of purity, while now several of them have reached their Iron Age, the *Kali Yuga,* an age black with horrors. This state will last . . . until we begin acting from within instead of ever following impulses from without. Until then the only palliative is union and harmony—a Brotherhood in *actu* and *altruism* not simply in name."

Edwin Arnold, in his wonderful poem, "The Light of Asia," which tells the story of the Buddha, explains the doctrine of Karma from the Buddhist standpoint. We feel that our students should become acquainted with this view, so beautifully expressed, and so we herewith quote the passages referred to:

"KARMA—all that total of a soul
  Which is the things it did, the thoughts it had,
The 'self' it wove with woof of viewless time
  Crossed on the warp invisible of acts.

. . . .

"What hath been bringeth what shall be, and is,
  Worse—better—last for first and first for last;
The angels in the heavens of gladness reap
  Fruits of a holy past.

"The devils in the underworlds wear out
  Deeds that were wicked in an age gone by.
Nothing endures: fair virtues waste with time,
  Foul sins grow purged thereby.

"Who toiled a slave may come anew a prince
For gentle worthiness and merit won;
Who ruled a king may wander earth in rags
For things done and undone.

"Before beginning, and without an end,
As space eternal and as surety sure,
Is fixed a Power divine which moves to good,
Only its laws endure.

"It will not be contemned of any one:
Who thwarts it loses, and who serves it gains;
The hidden good it pays with peace and bliss,
The hidden ill with pains.

"It seeth everywhere and marketh all:
Do right—it recompenseth! Do one wrong—
The equal retribution must be made,
Though DHARMA tarry long.

"It knows not wrath nor pardon; utter-true
Its measures mete, its faultless balance weighs;
Times are as naught, to-morrow it will judge,
Or after many days.

"By this the slayer's knife did stab himself;
The unjust judge hath lost his own defender;
The false tongue dooms its lie; the creeping thief
And spoiler rob, to render.

"Such is the law which moves to righteousness,
  Which none at last can turn aside or stay;
The heart of it is love, the end of it
  Is peace and consummation sweet. Obey!

. . . .

"The books say well, my brothers! each man's life
  The outcome of his former living is;
The bygone wrongs bring forth sorrow and woes,
  The bygone right breeds bliss.

"That which ye sow ye reap. See yonder fields!
  The sesamum was sesamum, the corn
Was corn. The silence and the darkness knew;
  So is a man's fate born.

"He cometh, reaper of the things he sowed,
  Sesamum, corn, so much cast in past birth;
And so much weed and poison-stuff, which mar
  Him and the aching earth.

"If he shall labor rightly, rooting these,
  And planting wholesome seedlings where they grew,
Fruitful and fair and clean the ground shall be,
  And rich the harvest due.

"If he who liveth, learning whence woe springs,
  Endureth patiently, striving to pay
His utmost debt for ancient evils done
  In love and truth alway;

"If making none to lack, he thoroughly purge
  The lie and lust of self forth from his blood;
Suffering all meekly, rendering for offence
  Nothing but grace and good:

"If he shall day by day dwell merciful,
  Holy and just and kind and true; and rend
Desire from where it clings with bleeding roots,
  Till love of life have end:

"He—dying—leaveth as the sum of him
  A life-count closed, whose ills are dead and quit,
Whose good is quick and mighty, far and near,
  So that fruits follow it.

"No need hath such to live as ye name life;
  That which began in him when he began
Is finished: he hath wrought the purpose through
  Of what did make him man.

"Never shall yearnings torture him, nor sins
  Stain him, nor ache of earthly joys and woes
Invade his safe eternal peace; nor deaths
  And lives recur. He goes

"Unto NIRVANA. He is one with Life
  Yet lives not. He is blest, ceasing to be.
OM, MANI PADME OM! the dewdrop slips
  Into the shining sea!

"This is the doctrine of the Karma. Learn!
  Only when all the dross of sin is quit,
Only when life dies like a white flame spent.
  Death dies along with it."

And so, friends, this is a brief account of the operations of the Law of Karma. The subject is one of such wide scope that the brief space at our disposal enables us to do little more than to call your attention to the existence of the Law, and some of its general workings. We advise our students to acquaint themselves thoroughly with what has been written on this subject by ourselves and others. In our first series of lessons—the *"Fourteen Lessons"*—the chapter or lesson on Spiritual Cause and Effect was devoted to the subject of Karma. We advise our students to re-study it. We also suggest that Mr. Sinnett's occult story entitled *"Karma"* gives its readers an excellent idea of the actual working of Karma in the everyday lives of people of our own times. We recommend the book to the consideration of our students. It is published at a popular price, and is well worth the consideration of every one interested in this wonderful subject of Reincarnation and Karma.

THE TWELFTH LESSON.

OCCULT MISCELLANY.

In this, the last lesson of this series, we wish to call your attention to a variety of subjects, coming under the general head of the Yogi Philosophy, and yet apparently separated from one another. And so we have entitled this lesson "Occult Miscellany," inasmuch as it is made up of bits of information upon a variety of subjects all connected with the general teaching of the series. The lesson will consist of answers to a number of questions, asked by various students of the courses in Yogi Philosophy coming from our pen. While these answers, of necessity, must be brief, still we will endeavor to condense considerable information into each, so that read as a whole the lesson will give to our students a variety of information upon several important subjects.

QUESTION I: *"Are there any Brotherhoods of Advanced Occultists in existence, in harmony with the Yogi Teachings? And if so, what information can you give regarding them?"*

ANSWER: Yes, there are a number of Occult Brotherhoods, of varying degrees of advancement, scattered through the various countries of the earth. These Brotherhoods agree in principle with the Yogi Teachings, although the methods of interpretation may vary somewhat. There is but one TRUTH, which becomes apparent to all deep students of Occultism, and therefore all true Occultists have a glimpse of that Truth, and upon this glimpse is founded their philosophies and teachings. These Occult Brotherhoods vary in their nature. In some, the members are grouped together in retired portions of the earth, dwelling in the community life. In others the headquarters are in the large cities of the earth, their membership being composed of residents of those cities, with outlying branches. Others have no meeting places, their work being managed from headquarters, their members being scattered all over the face of the earth, the communication being kept up by personal correspondence and privately printed and circulated literature. Admission to these true Occult Brotherhoods is difficult. They seek their members, not the members them. No amount of money, or influence, or energy can gain entrance to these societies. They seek to impart information and instruction only to those who are prepared to receive it—to those who have reached that stage of spiritual unfoldment that will enable them to grasp and assimilate the teachings of the Inner Circles. While this is true, it is also true that these Societies or Brotherhoods are engaged in disseminating Occult Knowledge, suited to the minds of the public, through various channels, and cloaked in various disguises of name, authority and style. Their idea is to gradually open the mind of the public to the great truths underlying and back of all of these various fragmentary teachings. And they recognize the fact that one mind may be reached in a certain way, and another mind in a second way, and so on. And, accordingly, they wrap their teachings in covers likely to attract the attention of various people, and to cause them to investigate the contents. But, under and back of all of these various teachings, is the great fundamental TRUTH. It has often been asked of us how one might distinguish the real Brotherhoods from the spurious ones which have assumed the name and general style of the true societies, for the purpose of exploiting the public, and making money from their interest in the great occult truths. Answering this, we would say that the true Occult Brotherhoods and Societies *never sell their knowledge.* It is given free as water to those who seek for it, and is never sold for money. The true adept would as soon think of selling his soul as selling Spiritual Knowledge for gain. While money plays its proper place in the world, and the laborer is worthy of his hire; and while the Masters recognize the propriety of the sale of books on Occultism (providing the price is reasonable and not in excess of the general market price of books) and while they also recognize the propriety of having people pay their part of the expenses of maintaining organizations, magazines, lecturers, instructors, etc., still the idea stops there—it does not extend to the selling of the Inner Secrets of Occultism for silver or gold. Therefore if you are solicited to become a member of any so-called Brotherhood or Occult Society for a consideration of money, you will know at once that the organization is not a true Occult Society, for it has violated one of the cardinal principles at the start. Remember the old occult maxim: "When the Pupil is ready, the Master appears"—and so it is with the Brotherhoods and Societies—if it is necessary for your growth, development, and attainment, to be connected with one of these organizations then, when the time comes—when you are ready—you will receive your call, and then will know for a certainty that those who call are the true messengers of Truth.

QUESTION II: *"Are there any exalted human beings called Masters, or Adepts, or are the tales regarding them mere fables, etc?"*

ANSWER: Of a truth there are certain highly developed, advanced and exalted souls in the flesh, known as Masters and Adepts, although many of the tales told concerning them are myths, or pure fiction originating in the minds of some modern sensational writers. And, moreover, these souls are members of the Great Lodge, an organization composed of these almost super-human beings—these great souls that have advanced so very far on THE PATH. Before beginning to sepak of them, let us answer a question often asked by Western people, and that is, "Why do not these people appear to the world, and show their powers?" Each of you may answer that question from your own experiences. Have you ever been foolish enough to open your soul to the crowd, and have it reveal the sacred Truth that rests there? Have you ever attempted to impart the highest teachings known to you, to persons who had not attained sufficient spiritual development to even understand the meaning of your words? Have you ever committed the folly of throwing spiritual pearls to material swine? If you have had these experiences, you may begin to faintly imagine the reasons of these illumined souls for keeping away from the crowd—for dwelling away from the multitude. No one who has not suffered the pain of having the vulgar crowd revile the highest spiritual truths to him, can begin to understand the feelings of the spiritually ilumined individuals. It is not that they feel that they are better or more exalted than the humblest man—for these feelings of the personality have long since left them. It is because they see the folly of attempting to present the highest truths to a public which is not prepared to understand even the elementary teachings. It is a feeling akin to that of the master of the highest musical conceptions attempting to produce his wonderful compositions before a crowd fit only for the "rag-time" and slangy songs of the day.

Then again, these Masters have no desire to "work miracles" which would only cause the public to become still more superstitious than they now are. When one glances back over the field of religions, and sees how the miraculous acts of some of the great leaders have been prostituted and used as a foundation for the grossest credulity and basest superstition, he may understand the wisdom of the masters in this respect. There is another reason for the non-appearance of the Masters, and that is that there is no occasion for it. The laws of Spiritual Evolution are as regular, constant and fixed as are the laws of Physical Evolution, and any attempt to unduly force matters only results in confusion, and the abortive results soon fade away. The world is not ready for the appearance of the Masters. Their appearance at this time would not be in accordance with The Plan.

The Masters or Adepts are human beings who have passed from lower to higher planes of consciousness, thus gaining wisdom, power and qualities that seem almost miraculous to the man of the ordinary consciousness. A Hindu writer speaking of them has said: "To him who hath traveled far along The Path, sorrow ceases to trouble; fetters cease to bind; obstacles cease to hinder. Such an one is free. For him there is no more fever or sorrow. For him there are no more unconscious re-births. His old Karma is exhausted, and he creates no new Karma. His heart is freed from the desire for future life. No new longings arise within his soul. He is like a lamp which burneth from the oil of the Spirit, and not from the oil of the outer world." Lillie in his work on Buddhism, tells his readers: "Six supernatural faculties were expected of the ascetic before he could claim the grade of *Arhat*. They are constantly alluded to in the *Sutras* as the six supernatural faculties, usually without further specification. . . . In this transitory body the intelligence of Man is enchained. The ascetic finding himself thus confused, directs his mind to the creation of *Manas*. He represents to himself, in thought, another body created from this material body,—a body with a form, members and organs. This body in relation to the material body is like a sword and the scabbard, or a serpent issuing from a basket in which it is confined. The ascetic then, purified and perfected, begins to practice supernatural faculties. He finds himself able to pass through material obstacles, walls, ramparts, etc.; he is able to throw his phantasmal appearance into many places at once. He acquires the power of hearing the sounds of the unseen world as distinctly as those of the phenomenal world—more distinctly in point of fact. Also by the power of *Manas* he is able to read the most secret thoughts of others, and to tell their characters."

These great Masters are above all petty sectarian distinctions. They may have ascended to their exalted position along the paths of the many religions, or they may have walked the path of no-denomination, sect, or body. They may have mounted to their heights by philosophical reasoning alone, or else by scientific investigation. They are called by many names, according to the viewpoint of the speaker, but at the last they are of but one religion; one philosophy; one belief—TRUTH.

The state of Adeptship is reached only after a long and arduous apprenticeship extending over many lives. Those who have reached the pinnacle were once even as You who read these lines. And some of you—yes, perhaps even You who are now reading these words may have taken the first steps along the narrow path which will lead you to heights equally as exalted as those occupied by even the highest of these great beings of whom we are speaking. Unconsciously to yourself, the urge of the Spirit has set your feet firmly upon The Path, and will push you forward to the end. In order to understand the occult custom that finds its full fruit in the seclusion of the Masters, one needs to be acquainted with the universal habit among true occultists of refraining from public or vulgar displays of occult power. While the inferior occultists often exhibit some of the minor manifestations to the public, it is a fact that the true advanced occultists scrupulously refrain from so doing. In fact, among the highest teachers, it is a condition imposed upon the pupil that he shall refrain from exhibitions of his developing powers among the uninitiated public. "The Neophyte is bound over to the most inviolable secrecy as to everything connected with his entrance and further progress in the schools. In Asia, in the same way, the *chela,* or pupil of occultism, no sooner becomes a *chela* than he ceases to be a witness on behalf of the reality of occult knowledge," says Sinnett in his great work on "Esoteric Buddhism," And he then adds: "I have been astonished to find, since my own connection with the subject, how numerous such *chelas* are. But it is impossible to imagine any human act more improbable than the unauthorized revelation by any such *chela,* to persons in the outer world, that he is one; and so the great esoteric school of philosophy guards its seclusion."

QUESTION III: *"Does the Yogi Philosophy teach that there is a place corresponding to the 'Heavens' of the various religions? Is there any basis for the belief that there is a place resembling 'Heaven'?"*

ANSWER: Yes, the Yogi Philosophy *does* teach that there is a real basis for the popular religious beliefs in "Heaven," and that there are states of being, the knowledge of which has filtered through to the masses in the more or less distorted theories regarding "heavens."

But the Yogis do not teach that these "heavens" are *places* at all. The teaching is that they are *planes of existence*. It is difficult to explain just what is meant by this word "plane." The nearest approach to it in English is the term or word "State." A portion of space may be occupied by several planes at the same time, just as a room may be filled with the rays of the sun, those of a lamp, X-rays, magnetic and electric vibrations and waves, etc., each interpenetrating each other and yet not affecting or interfering with each other.

On the lower planes of the Astral World there are to be found the earth-bound souls which have passed out from their former bodies, but which are attracted to the earthly scenes by strong attractions, which serve to weight them down and to prevent them from ascending to the higher planes. On the higher planes are souls that are less bound by earthly attractions, and who, accordingly, are relieved of the weight resulting therefrom. These planes rise in an ascending scale, each plane being higher and more spiritual than the one lower than itself. And dwelling on each plane are the souls fitted to occupy it, by reason of their degree of spiritual development, or evolution. When the soul first leaves the body it falls into a sleep-like stage, from which it awakens to find itself on the plane for which it is fitted, by reason of its development, attractions, character, etc. The particular plane occupied by each soul is determined by the progress and attainment it has made in its past lives. The souls on the higher planes may, and often do, visit the planes lower in the scale than their own, but those on the lower planes may not visit those higher than their own. Quoting from our own writings on this subject, published several years ago, we repeat: This prohibition regarding the visiting of higher planes is not an arbitrary rule, but a law of nature. If the student will pardon the commonplace comparison, he may get an understanding of it, by imagining a large screen, or series of screens, such as used for sorting coal into sizes. The large coal is caught by the first screen; the next size by the second; and so on until the tiny coal is reached. Now, the large coal cannot get into the receptacle of the smaller sizes, but the small sizes may easily pass through the screen and join the larger sizes, if force be imparted to them. Just so in the Astral World, the soul with the greatest amount of materiality, and gross nature, is stopped by the spiritual screen of a certain plane, and cannot pass on to the higher ones, while other souls have cast off some of the confining and retarding material sheaths, and readily pass on to higher and finer planes. And it may be readily seen that those souls which dwell on the higher planes are able to re-visit the lower and grosser planes, while the souls on the grosser cannot penetrate the higher boundries of their plane, being stopped by the spiritual screen. The comparison is a crude one, but it almost exactly pictures the existing conditions on the spiritual world.

Souls on the upper planes, may, and often do, journey to the lower planes for the purpose of "visiting" the souls of friends who may be dwelling there, and thus affording them comfort and consolation. In fact, the teaching is that in many cases a highly developed soul visits souls on the lower planes in whom it is interested, and actually imparts spiritual teaching and instruction to those souls, so that they may be re-born into much better conditions than would have been the case otherwise. All of the planes have Spiritual Instructors from very high planes, who sacrifice their well-earned rest and happiness on their own planes in order that they may work for the less-developed souls on the lower planes.

As we have said, the soul awakens on the plane to which it is suited. It finds itself in the company of congenial souls, in whose company it is enabled to pursue those things which were dear to its heart when alive. It may be able to make considerable advancement during its sojourn in "heaven," which will result to its benefit when it is reborn on earth. There are countless sub-planes, adapted to the infinite requirements of the advancing souls in every degree of development, and each soul finds an opportunity to develop and enjoy to the fullest the highest of which it is capable, and to also perfect itself and to prepare itself for future development, so that it may be re-born under the very best possible conditions and circumstances in the next earth life. But, alas, even in this higher world, all souls do not live up to the best that is in them, and instead of making the best of their opportunities for development, and growing spiritually, they allow the attractions of their material natures to draw them downward, and too often spend much of their time on the planes beneath them, not to help and assist, but to live the less spiritual lives of their friends on the lower planes. In such cases the soul does not reap the benefit of the sojourn in the "after-life," but is born again according to the attractions of its lower, instead of its higher nature, and is compelled to learn its lesson over again.

The Yogi teachings inform us that the lower planes of the Astral World are inhabited by souls of a very gross and degraded type, undeveloped and animal-like. These low souls live out the tendencies and characteristics of their former earth lives, and reincarnate rapidly in order to pursue their material attractions. Of course, there is slowly working even in these undeveloped souls an upward tendency, but it is so slow as to be almost imperceptible. In time these undeveloped souls grow sick and tired of their materiality, and then comes the chance for a slight advance. Of course these undeveloped souls have no access to the higher planes of the Astral world, but are confined to their own degraded plane and to the sub-planes which separate the Astral World from the material world. They cling as closely as possible to the earthly scenes, and are separated from the material world by only a thin screen (if we may use the word). They suffer the tantalizing condition of being within sight and hearing of their old material scenes and environments, and yet unable to manifest on them. These souls form the low class of "spirits" of which we hear so much in certain circles. They hang around their old scenes of debauchery and sense gratification, and often are able to influence the minds of living persons along the same line and plane of development. For instance, these creatures hover around low saloons and places of ill-repute, influencing the sodden brains of living persons to participate in the illicit gratifications of the lower sensual nature.

Souls on the higher planes are not bound by these earthly and material attractions, and take advantage of their opportunities to improve themselves and develop spiritually. It is a rule of the Astral World that the higher the plane occupied by a soul, the longer the sojourn there between incarnations. A soul on the lowest planes may reincarnate in a very short time, while on the higher planes hundreds and even thousands of years may elapse before the soul is called upon to experience re-birth. But re-birth comes to all who have not passed on to other spheres of life. Sooner or later the soul feels that inward urge toward re-birth and further experience, and becomes drowsy and falls into a state resembling sleep, when it is caught up in the current that is sweeping on toward re-birth, and is gradually carried on to re-birth in conditions chosen by its desires and characteristics, in connection with the operation of the laws of Karma. From the soul-slumber it passes through what may be called a "death" on the Astral plane, when it is re-born on the earth plane. But, remember this, the soul, when it is re-born on earth, does not fully awaken from its Astral sleep. In infancy and in early childhood the soul is but slowly awakening, gradually from year to year, the brain being built to accommodate this growth. The rare instances of precocious children, and infant genius are cases in which the awakening has been more rapid than ordinary. On the other hand, cases are known where the soul does not awaken as rapidly as the average, and the result is that the person does not show signs of full intellectual activity until nearly middle age. Cases are known when men seemed to "wake up" when they were forty years of age, or even later in life, and would then take on a freshened activity and energy, surprising those who had known them before.

On some of the planes of the Astral world the souls dwelling there do not seem to realize that they are "dead," but act and live as if they were in the flesh.

They have a knowledge of the planes beneath them, just as we on earth know of conditions beneath us (spiritually), but they seem to be in almost absolute ignorance of the planes above them, just as many of us on earth cannot comprehend the existence of beings more highly developed spiritually than ourselves. This, of course, is only true of the souls who have not been made acquainted with the meaning and nature of life on the Astral Plane. Those who have acquired this information and knowledge readily understand their condition and profit thereby. It will be seen from this that it is of the greatest importance for persons to become acquainted with the great laws of Occultism in their present earth life, for the reason that when they pass out of the body and enter some one of the Astral Planes they will not be in ignorance of the condition, but will readily grasp the meaning and nature of their surroundings and take advantage of the same in order to develop themselves more rapidly.

It will be seen from what has been written by us here and elsewhere that there are planes after planes on the Astral side of life. All that has been dreamt of Heaven, Purgatory or Hell has its correspondence there, although not in the literal sense in which these things have been taught. For instance, a wicked man dying immersed in his desires and longings of his lower nature, and believing that he will be punished in a future life for sins committed on earth—such a one is very apt to awaken on the lower planes or sub-planes, in conditions corresponding with his former fears. He finds the fire and brimstone awaiting him, although these things are merely figments of his own imagination, and having no existence in reality. Murderers may roam for ages (apparently) pursued by the bleeding corpses of their victims, until such a horror of the crime arises in the mind that at last sinking from exhaustion into the soul-sleep, their souls pass into re-birth with such a horror of bloodshed and crime as to make them entirely different beings in the new life. And, yet the "hell" that they went through existed only in their imaginations. They were their own Devil and Hell. Just as a man in earth life may suffer from *delirium tremens,* so some of these souls on the Astral plane suffer agonies from their delirium arising from their former crimes, and the belief in the punishment therefor which has been inculcated in them through earth teachings. And these mental agonies, although terrible, really are for their benefit, for by reason of them the soul becomes so sickened with the thought and idea of crime that when it is finally re-born it manifests a marked repulsion to it, and flies to the opposite. In this connection we would say that the teaching is that although the depraved soul apparently experiences ages of this torment, yet, in reality, there is but the passage of but a short time, the illusion arising from the self-hypnotization of the soul, just as arises the illusion of the punishment itself.

In the same way the soul often experiences a

"heaven" in accordance with its hopes, beliefs and longings of earth-life. The "heaven" that it has longed for and believed in during its earth-life is very apt to be at least partially reproduced on the Astral plane, and the pious soul of any and all religious denominations finds itself in a "heaven" corresponding to that in which it believed during its earth-life. The Mohammedan finds his paradise; the Christian finds his; the Indian finds his—but the impression is merely an illusion created by the Mental Pictures of the soul. But the illusion tends to give pleasure to the soul, and to satisfy certain longings which in time fade away, leaving the soul free to reach out after higher conceptions and ideals. We cannot devote more space to this subject at this time, and must content ourselves with the above statements and explanations. The principal point that we desire to impress upon your minds is the fact that the "heaven-world" is not a place or state of permanent rest and abode for the disembodied soul, but is merely a place or temporary sojourn between incarnations, and thus serves as a place of rest wherein the soul may gather together its forces, energies, desires and attractions preparatory to re-birth. In this answer we have merely limited ourselves to a general statement of the states and conditions of the Astral World, or rather of certain planes of that world. The subject itself requires far more extensive treatment.

QUESTION IV: *"Is Nirvana a state of the total extinction of consciousness; and is it a place, state or condition?"*

ANSWER: The teaching concerning *Nirvana*, the final goal of the soul, has been much misunderstood, and much error has crept into the teaching even among some very worthy teachers. To conceive of *Nirvana* as a state of extinction of consciousness would be to fall into the error of the pessimistic school of philosophy which thinks of life and consciousness as a curse, and regards the return into a total unconsciousness as the thing to be most desired. The true teaching is that *Nirvana* is a state of the fullest consciousness—a state in which the soul is relieved of all the illusion of separateness and relativity, and enters into a state of Universal Consciousness, or Absolute Awareness, in which it is conscious of Infinity, and Eternity—of all places and things and time. *Nirvana* instead of being a state of Nothingness, is a state of "Everythingness." As the soul advances along the Path it becomes more and more aware of its connection with, relation to, and identity with the Whole. As it grows, the Self enlarges and transcends its former limited bounds. It begins to realize that it is more than the tiny separated atom that it had believed itself to be, and it learns to identify itself in a constantly increasing scale with the Universal Life. It feels a sense of Oneness in a fuller degree, and it sets its feet firmly upon the Path toward *Nirvana*. After many weary lives on this and other planets—in this and other Universes—after it has long since left behind it the scale of humanity, and has advanced into god-like states, its consciousness becomes fuller and fuller, and time and space are transcended in a wonderful manner. And at last the goal is attained—the battle is won—and the soul blossoms into a state of Universal Consciousness, in which Time and Place disappear and in which every place is Here; every period of Time is Now; and everything is "I." This is *Nirvana.*

QUESTION V: *"What is that which Occultists call 'an Astral Shell,' or similar name? Is it an entity, or force, or being?"*

ANSWER: When the soul passes out from the body at the moment of death it carries with it the "Astral Body" as well as the higher mental and spiritual principles (see the first three lessons in the "Fourteen Lessons"). The Astral Body is the counterpart of the material or physical body, although it is composed of matter of a much finer and ethereal nature than is the physical body. It is invisible to the ordinary eye, but may be seen clairvoyantly. The Astral Body rises from the physical body like a faint, luminous vapor, and for a time is connected with the dying physical body by a thin, vapory cord or thread, which finally breaks entirely and the separation becomes complete. The Astral Body is some time afterward discarded by the soul as it passes on to the higher planes, as we have described a few pages further back, and the abandoned Astral Body becomes an "Astral Shell," and is subject to a slow disintegration, just as is the physical body. It is no more the soul than is the physical body—it is merely a cast off garment of fine matter. It will be seen readily that it is not an entity, force or being—

it is only cast off matter—a sloughed skin. It has no life or intelligence, but floats around on the lower Astral Plane until it finally disintegrates. It has an attraction toward its late physical associate—the physical body—and often returns to the place where the latter is buried, where it is sometimes seen by persons whose astral sight is temporarily awakened, when it is mistaken for a "ghost" or "spirit" of the person. These Astral Shells are often seen floating around over graveyards, battlefields, etc. And sometimes these shells coming in contact with the psychic magnetism of a medium become "galvanized" into life, and manifest signs of intelligence, which, however, really comes from the mind of the medium. At some seances these re-vitalized shells manifest and materialize, and talk in a vague, meaningless manner, the shell receiving its vitality from the body and mind of the medium instead of speaking from any consciousness of its own. This statement is not to be taken as any denial of true "spirit return," but is merely an explanation of certain forms of so-called "spiritualistic phenomena" which is well understood by advanced "spiritualists," although many seekers after psychic phenomena are in ignorance of it.

QUESTION VI: *What is meant by "the Days and Nights of Brahm"; the "Cycles"; the "Chain of Worlds", etc., etc.?*

ANSWER: In Lesson Sixth, of the present series, you will find a brief mention of the "Days and Nights of Brahm"—those vast periods of the Inbreathing and Outbreathing of the Creative Principle which is personified in the Hindu conception of *Brahma.* You will see mentioned there that universal philosophical conception of the Universal Rhythm, which manifests in a succession of periods of Universal Activity and Inactivity.

The Yogi Teachings are that all Time is manifested in Cycles. Man calls the most common form of Cyclic Time by the name of "a Day," which is the period of time necessary for the earth's revolution on its axis. Each Day is a reproduction of all previous Days, although the incidents of each day differ from those of the other—all Days are but periods of Time marked off by the revolution of the earth on its axis. And each Night is but the negative side of a Day, the positive side of which is called "day." There is really no such thing as a Day, that which we call a "Day" being simply a record of certain physical changes in the earth's position relating to its own axis.

The second phase of Cyclic Time is called by man by the name "a Month," by which is meant certain changes in the relative positions of the moon and the earth. The true month consists of twenty-eight lunar days. In this Cycle (the Month) there is also a light-time or "day," and a dark-time or "night," the former being the fourteen days of the moon's visibility, and the second being the fourteen days of the moon's invisibility.

The third phase of Cyclic Time is that which we call "a Year," by which is meant the time occupied by the earth in its revolution around the sun. You will notice that the year has its positive and negative periods, also, known as Summer and Winter.

But the Yogis take up the story where the astronomers drop it, at the Year. Beyond the Year there are other and greater phases of Cyclic Time. The Yogis know many cycles of thousands of years in which there are marked periods of Activity and Inactivity. We cannot go into detail regarding these various cycles, but may mention another division common to the Yogi teachings, beginning with the Great Year. The Great Year is composed of 360 earth years. Twelve thousand Great Years constitute what is known as a Great Cycle, which is seen to consist of 4,320,000 earth years. Seventy-one Great Cycles compose what is called a *Manwantara,* at the end of which the earth becomes submerged under the waters, until not a vestige of land is left uncovered. This state lasts for a period equal to 71 Great Cycles. A *Kalpa* is composed of 14 Manwantaras. The largest and grandest Cycle manifested is known as the *Maya-Praylaya,* consisting of 36,000 *Kalpas* when the Absolute withdraws into Itself its entire manifestations, and dwells alone in its awful Infinity and Oneness, this period being succeeded by a period equally long—the two being known as the Days and Nights of Brahm.

You will notice that each of these great Cycles has its "Day" period and its "Night" period—its Period of Activity and its Period of Inactivity. From Day to Maya-Praylaya, it is a succession of Nights and Days—Creative Activity and Creative Cessation.

The "Chain of Worlds," is that great group of planets in our own solar system, seven in number, over which the Procession of Life passes, in Cycles. From globe to globe the great wave of soul life passes in Cyclic Rhythm. After a race has passed a certain number of incarnations upon one planet, it passes on to another, and learns new lessons, and then on and on until finally it has learned all of the lessons possible on this Universe, when it passes on to another Universe, and so on, from higher to higher until the human mind is unable to even think of the grandeur of the destiny awaiting each human soul on THE PATH. The various works published by the Theosophical organizations go into detail regarding these matters, which require the space of many volumes to adequately express, but we think that we have at last indicated the general nature of the question, pointing out to the student the nature of the subject, and indicating lines for further study and investigation.

CONCLUSION.

And now, dear students, we have reached the end of this series of lessons. You have followed us closely for the past four years, many of you having been with us as students from the start. We feel many ties of spiritual relationship binding you to us, and the parting, although but temporary, gives a little pang to us—a little pull upon our heart strings. We have tried to give to you a plain, practical and simple exposition of the great truths of this world-old philosophy—have endeavored to express in plain simple terms the greatest truths known to man on earth to-day, *the Yogi Philosophy*. And many have written us that our work has not been in vain, and that we have been the means of opening up new worlds of thought to them, and have aided them in casting off the old material sheaths that had bound them for so long, and the discarding of which enabled them to unfold the beautiful blossom of Spirituality. Be this as it may, we have been able merely to give you the most elementary instruction in this world-philosophy, and are painfully conscious of the small portion of the field that we have tilled, when compared with the infinite expanse of Truth still untouched. But such are the limitations of Man—he can speak only of that which lies immediately before him, leaving for others the rest of the work which is remote from his place of abode. There are planes upon planes of this Truth which every soul among you will some day make his or her own. It is yours, and you will be impelled to reach forth and take that which is intended for you. Be not in too much haste—be of great patience—and all will come to you, for it is your own.

"MYSTIC CHRISTIANITY."

We have here to make an announcement that will please our readers, judging from the many letters that we have received during the several years of our work. We will now enter upon a new phase of our work of presenting the great truths underlying life, as taught by the great minds of centuries ago, and carefully transmitted from master to student from that time unto our own. We have concluded our presentation of the mystic teachings underlying the Hindu Philosophies, and shall now pass on to a consideration and presentation of the great Mystic Principles underlying that great and glorious creed of the Western world—the religion, teachings, and philosophy of JESUS THE CHRIST. These teachings, too, as we should remember, are essentially Eastern in their origin, and source, although their effects are more pronounced in the Western world. Underlying the teaching and philosophy of the Christ are to be found the same esoteric principles that underlie the other great systems of philosophies of the East. Covered up though the Truth be by the additions of the Western churches and sects, still it remains there burning brightly as ever, and plainly visible to one who will brush aside the rubbish surrounding the Sacred Flame and who will seek beneath the forms and non-essentials for the Mystic Truths underlying Christianity.

We realize the importance of the work before us, but we shrink not from the task, for we know that when the bright Light of the Spirit, which is found as the centre of the Christian philosophy, is uncovered, there will be great rejoicing from the many who while believing in and realizing the value of the Eastern Teachings, still rightly hold their love, devotion and admiration for Him who was in very Truth the Son of God, and whose mission was to raise the World spiritually from the material quagmire into which it was stumbling.

And now, dear pupils, we must close this series of lessons on the Yogi Philosophy. We must rest ere we so soon engage upon our new and great work. We must each take a little rest, ere we meet again on The Path of Attainment. Each of these temporary partings are milestones upon our Journey of Spiritual Life. Let each find us farther advanced.

And now we send you our wishes of Peace. May The Peace be with you all, now and forever, even unto NIRVANA, which is PEACE itself.